# CHILDREN OF GOD

# CHILDREN OF GOD

*The Life of Spiritual Childhood*
*Preached by Saint Josemaría Escrivá*

FRANCIS FERNANDEZ-CARVAJAL
*and*
PETER BETETA

TRANSLATED BY DENNIS M. HELMING

 Scepter

First published as *Hijos de Dios.*
Original Spanish edition copyright © 1997, Ediciones Palabra, S.A., Madrid.

English translation copyright © 1997 by
Scepter Publishers, Inc., P.O. Box 211, New York, NY 10018.
www.scepterpublishers.org

ISBN 1–889334–05–7

Third printing, 2005

Printed in the United States of America

# Contents

## Part Two: Behavior Befitting Children of God

# Foreword

In 1981 from the pen of Fernando Ocariz came *God as Father in the Message of Blessed Josemaría Escrivá.*[1] In its pages countless people, both theologians and lay people, told of the lasting impression left by the spiritual legacy of Opus Dei's founder. It brought to light the question of what contribution to theological development was made by this holy priest.

Following its format and suggestions, this book, aimed at a broader public, deals with the theme of divine filiation and its influence on Christian living. We also incorporate some previously unpublished texts. While acknowledging the challenge of deciphering the divine mystery, we seek to clarify with both word and example the theological concepts that are at the very core of Christian existence.

## A never-exhausted reality

The first successor of Blessed Josemaría, then Msgr. Alvaro del Portillo, wrote in the foreword to a book of the former's homilies: "Note, for example, how the author comments on the Gospel. He never simply brings it in for show or in a hackneyed way. Each verse has been meditated frequently and yields new aspects hidden, perhaps, for centuries."[2]

Undoubtedly one of the new aspects long hidden is an awareness of divine filiation. Not just one among many theoretical truths, it is to be contemplated and lived as the axis on which turns all Christian existence, a truth that continues to

---

[1] The Spanish original appeared in *Scripta Theologica,* vol. 13, 161ff. The English translation is *God As Father* (Princeton, NJ: Scepter, 1995).

[2] Josemaría Escrivá, *Christ Is Passing By,* p. 10.

grow to the extent that it guides our steps. Proclaiming it from the housetops, as an essential strain of the Gospel,[3] soon leads to the transformation of life that so many Church Fathers championed.

Blessed Josemaría's life and teachings reveal how central was his sense of being a child of God. Early in *The Way* we read: " 'Father,' said that big fellow, a good student at the University (I wonder what has become of him), 'I was thinking of what you told me—that I'm a son of God!—and I found myself walking along the street, head up, chin out, and a feeling of pride inside . . . a son of God!' With sure conscience I advised him to foster that *pride.*"[4]

Blessed Josemaría often spoke of the holy pride of a good child. He would insist on a Christian having as a leading feature what he called "good godliness." By that he meant the humility of recognizing the great truth that we are children of God. Thus he would say: "Draw strength from your divine filiation. God is a Father—your Father!—full of warmth and infinite love. Call him Father frequently and tell him, when you are alone, that you love him, that you love him very much, and that you feel proud and strong because you are his child."[5]

By declaring this priest blessed, the Church has also recognized the "new light" of divine filiation as a providential gift Opus Dei's founder was to spread: "The new blessed's spiritual and apostolic life," declared the Roman Pontiff, "rested on his knowing himself through faith to be God's son in Christ."[6] We are children of God! God especially endowed Blessed Josemaría to make this new light an everyday reality.

In another foreword, del Portillo noted that Escrivá's sole role was "to pray and to encourage others to do likewise. That was why he brought about in the midst of the world a wonderful 'mobilization of people,' as he liked to call it, 'who are ready to commit themselves to live Christian lives,' by developing their filial relationship with God our Father. Many of us have learned, from this thoroughly priestly priest, 'the great secret of God's

[3] In the four Gospels alone, some 133 references are made to God's fatherhood and, consequently, to divine filiation as the heart of Christian life.

[4] Josemaría Escrivá, *The Way*, no. 274.

[5] Josemaría Escrivá, *The Forge*, no. 331.

[6] John Paul II, Homily, beatification Mass on May 17, 1992.

mercy: that we are children of God.'"[7] He labels it a secret, a great secret stemming from God's unending mercy. The mystery of God's love for humanity is rooted in our condition as children of God.

## Bedrock for Christian living

Blessed Escrivá saw in divine filiation the foundation for the task of our sanctification. So says del Portillo: "What basis, what grounds do Christians have for nurturing such amazing aspirations in their lives? The answer comes as a sort of refrain, again and again, right through these homilies: it is the humble sense of daring 'of the person who, knowing himself to be poor and weak, knows also that he is a child of God.'"[8]

"Monsignor Escrivá sees a clear alternative facing every human being: 'slavery or divine sonship, this is the dilemma we face. Children of God or slaves to pride.'"[9]

When we freely come to depend on God for everything, by lovingly dwelling on our divine filiation, false dependence and anguish disappear, along with fears in the face of hardships and excessive concern for security. "There is nothing better than recognizing that Love has made us slaves of God. From the moment we recognize this, we cease being slaves and become friends, children."[10]

This living as children of God always and everywhere pervades Blessed Josemaría's preaching. Thus, in always speaking of God, he does so as a child who wants nothing more than that others be made aware of this beautiful, childlike relationship. He thereby often echoed the Apostle [Paul]: "For all who are led by the Spirit of God are sons of God. For you did not receive the spirit of slavery to fall back into fear, but you have received the spirit of sonship. When we cry, 'Abba, Father!' it is the Spirit himself bearing witness with our spirit that we are children of God, and if children, then heirs, heirs of God and fellow heirs

[7] Josemaría Escrivá, *Friends of God*, x; Getting to know God, no. 145.
[8] *Friends of God*, xii; Humility, no. 108.
[9] *Friends of God*, xii; Freedom, a gift from God, no. 38.
[10] *Friends of God*, no. 35.

with Christ, provided we suffer with him in order that we may also be glorified with him" (Rom 8: 14-17).

Our dignity as children of God is so radical that it transforms from within every Christian endeavor amid the world. Our activity becomes the deeds of God's offspring. "Divine filiation is a joyful truth, a consoling mystery. It fills all our spiritual life, it shows us how to speak to God, to know and love our Father in heaven. And it makes our interior struggle overflow with hope and gives us the trusting simplicity of little children. More than that: precisely because we are children of God, we can contemplate in love and wonder everything as coming from the hands of our Father, God the Creator. And so we become contemplatives in the middle of the world, loving the world." [11]

Opus Dei members, ordinary Christians who become closer to God by pursuing secular affairs, seek to have their lives permeated with this filiation, wherever they find themselves. From the outset their founder claimed: "This divine filiation is the basis of the spirit of Opus Dei." [12]

## A new discovery

God profoundly etched in Blessed Josemaría's soul, at a very precise moment, the realization of divine filiation. It happened in autumn of 1931, while on a trolley in Madrid, when Opus Dei was barely three years old. Hardships and misunderstandings were raining down on the young founder, who, far from capsizing, took confident refuge in his Father God. The result was a much keener and reinforced sense of being God's son, with a precision that later he would often recall. [13] "When the Lord

[11] *Christ Is Passing By*, no. 65.

[12] Ibid., no. 64.

[13] He himself refers to it in a personal log: "I was considering God's kindnesses towards me, and, full of interior joy, I would have cried out in the street, so that the whole world might know of my filial gratitude: Father, Father! And if not shouting, at least under my breath I walked about calling upon him in that way [Father!], certain that I was pleasing him." *Intimate Notes*, no. 296, quoted by A. de Fuenmayor, V. Gomez-Iglesias, and J. L. Illanes, *The Canonical Path of Opus Dei*, 26.

A few days later the same sentiments made themselves felt, while a phrase from Scripture was branded on his soul: "You are my son" (Ps 2: 7). These inspired gave me those blows around 1931, I did not understand. And suddenly in the midst of that great bitterness the words, *You are my son* (Ps 2: 7), you are Christ. And I only knew how to say, *Abba, Pater! Abba, Pater! Abba! Abba! Abba!* Now I see it with new light, as a new discovery, just as with the passage of time one sees the Lord's hand, the wisdom of the Almighty. You have made me understand, Lord, that to have the cross is to find happiness and joy. And the reason—I see it more clearly now than ever— is this: to have the cross is to identify oneself with Christ, to be Christ, and for this reason to be God's child." [14] These and other texts, from long ago, reflect what was that "new light, like a new discovery" for Opus Dei's founder.

The novelty grasped by his soul as a result of these happenings in 1931 was the intimate connection between divine filiation and experience of the cross. The source and content of bliss lie in Christ's cross. Only in this way is one identified with Christ and is, therefore, a child of God. So does God the Father relate to his adopted children. "[T]o imitate Christ, and be good disciples of his, we must take his advice to heart, 'If any man has a mind to come my way, let him deny himself and take up his cross and follow me' (Mt 16: 24)." [15] "*In laetitia, nulla dies sine cruce!* I like to repeat with my soul filled with joy, there is not a single day without a cross—*the* cross." [16]

The experience of so many years of dedication and priestly work confirmed for Blessed Josemaría what God had shown him at the start of his calling to be Opus Dei's founder: Both trying circumstances and sacrifice, often opaque to the mind, are privileged chances to manifest our condition as God's children.

---

words, doubtlessly meditated upon many times before, quickly took on new meaning, with an unexpected light. Then, as he recounts, "I felt the Lord's action, germinating in my heart and on my lips, with the light of something wholly overwhelming, the tender invocation: *Abba, Pater.*" *Letter*, January 9, 1959. Flooded with joy, inebriated as it were by the awareness of his divine sonship, he experienced with absolute certainty: I am God's son! The spontaneous response broke forth, again with words from scripture: *Abba, Pater! Abba, Abba, Abba!* Then, as he mentions in *Intimate Notes*, no. 334: "Prayer surged up in me with copious and ardent affections."

[14] Meditation, April 28, 1963, cited by Alvaro del Portillo, *On Priesthood*.

[15] *Friends of God*, no. 216.

[16] *Christ Is Passing By*, no. 176.

He thoroughly understood, in faith's light, that to live as good children and to be united to the Father and the Holy Spirit, one must identify oneself with Jesus on the cross. "I have been crucified with Christ; it is no longer I who live, but Christ who lives in me" (Gal 2: 20). "To be an apostle you have to bear within you Christ crucified, as Saint Paul teaches us." [17] "It's true: when the holy cross comes into our lives it unmistakably confirms that we are his, Christ's." [18]

We can consider Escrivá's love for the cross as one of his defining features. Yet he did not just accept it as another manifestation of God's will. To correspond to divine requirements, he strove continually to seek the cross, within a generous spirit of penance. Thus did he become "a habitual dweller on Calvary." [19]

This goal is open to every Christian. As St. Thomas claims, "By dying with Christ on the cross and by being resurrected with him, 'I live' (that is to say, I have acquired a new power for doing good), but 'no longer I' (not according to the flesh, since sin has been expunged). Rather, *vivit in me Christus:* there lives in me a new life, that obtained by Christ." [20] Accordingly, Blessed Josemaría did not hesitate to ask trustingly for this gift: "Make the foundation of my personality my identification with you." [21] "Jesus, I want to be a blazing fire of Love-madness. I want it to be sufficient for me just to be present in order to set the world on fire for miles around, with an unquenchable flame. I want to know that I am yours. Then, let the cross come. . . ." [22] Owing to his contemplative familiarity with Christ, God the Father lovingly led him along the way of cherishing suffering and the cross.

---

[17] *The Forge*, no. 786.

[18] Ibid., no. 787.

[19] So was he described by an official of the Vatican Congregation for the Causes of Saints preparatory to his being declared "blessed." *Josemaría Escrivá de Balaguer: Itinerario de la Causa de Canonización* (Madrid, 1992), 41.

[20] Thomas Aquinas, *Commentary on the Epistle to the Galatians*, no. 106.

[21] *Christ Is Passing By*, no. 31.

[22] *The Forge*, no. 790.

# Our purpose

Our proposed task, that of gleaning Escrivá's "instinct" for divine filiation from his writings, is, in the words of Fernando Ocáriz, both "easy and demanding." Easy, because the texts, "despite their depth, display uncommon lucidity and powerful spiritual incisiveness. There's no need to 'interpret' them, even less to carve them up, thereby draining them of life." On the other hand, the task will be trying, "because in fact divine filiation impregnates everything he did and said. The quest cannot be limited to particular sections of his writings, however numerous. One cannot merely track down references to 'divine filiation' or its equivalents. When Escrivá speaks of faith, his is the faith of God's children. . . . Every virtue, every Christian (and even human) dimension, is, for him, that of God's children. Moreover, all his teaching, especially that born of contemplative savoring, defies categorization, any rationalistic dissection." [23]

Let these pages be a commentary on the fundamental reality lived and spread by Blessed Josemaría: the experiential knowledge he had of his condition as a son of God. Therein we will also glimpse, correlatively,* the riches of his soul. His was a unity of the divine and the human, patterned on Christ's simplicity: that of a child of God.

The following pages contain many of his quotations dealing with this human–divine filial relationship, arranged according to a minimal framework. Ours is not a work of theological research, but of compilation and commentary. May it thereby help readers to meditate on this great Christian mystery.

* correspondingly

filiation: relationship between parents & their children

filial

[23] *Vivir como hijos de Dios,* 24.

# Part One

# BEING CHILDREN OF GOD

# CHAPTER I

# God's Designs for Humanity

## The human creature's dignity

God's infinite goodness towers over all creation, while sustaining it. "Our faith teaches us that all creation, the earth's movement and that of other heavenly bodies, the good actions of creatures and all the good that has been achieved in history—in short everything comes from God and is directed toward him."[1] This is the initial truth upon which all else must rest.

Within the material creation, man occupies the top rung, in God's eyes. We can begin to get an idea of the dignity of human nature when we consider that God so loved us as to make us in his image and likeness. The Church never ceases to proclaim that man is the only being within physical creation that God loves for its own sake, for what it is in itself. Dwelling on God's merciful love for each of us easily spills over into thanksgiving and overwhelming joy.[2]

God has created men and women to give him glory, to be the instrument that interprets and proclaims to others, to all of

---

[1] *Christ Is Passing By*, no. 130.

[2] This truth often led Blessed Josemaría to show his grateful joy for divine love: "We have learned with gratitude, because it makes us realize the happiness we are being called to, that all creatures have been created out of nothing by God and for God: both men, who are rational creatures, although we so often act unreasonably, and the irrational beings, who roam the face of the earth, or burrow in its innermost recesses, or sail the azure skies—some soaring so high that they come face to face with the sun. But in all this wonderful variety, it is only we men (I am not now referring to the angels) who can unite ourselves to the Creator by using our freedom. We are in a position to give him, or deny him, the glory that is his due as the Author of everything that exists. . . . This hymn to freedom is echoed in all the mysteries of our Catholic faith. The blessed Trinity draws the world and man out of nothing, in a free outpouring of love." *Friends of God*, nos. 24–25.

creation, the endless beauty of God's glory. It is in this way that humans reach personal bliss.

Humanity's peerless dignity is already present in its origin, but with the incarnation of the Word, the Word's betrothal with human nature,[3] that dignity reaches its complete manifestation.[4] Truly "our commonwealth is in heaven, and from it we await a Savior, the Lord Jesus Christ, who will change our lowly body to be like his glorious body, by the power that enables him even to subject all things to himself" (Phil 3: 20–21).

## Called to intimacy with God

Man is, however, much more than God's favored creature. God has called him to an end completely beyond his natural powers. By the mystery of his love, a mere corner of its veil do we fleetingly lift, "we have been called to penetrate the intimacy of God's own life, to know and love God the Father, God the Son, and God the Holy Spirit, and to love also—in that same love of the one God in three divine Persons—the angels and all men."[5]

God, subsistent Love that makes man in his own image, has endowed us with the ability to know our maker. "And he can love God, who opens heaven's gates to us, makes us members of his family, and allows us to talk to him in friendship, face to face."[6] We could never have imagined such trust.

Our divine destiny is tied up with God's infinite and eternal wisdom. God conceived us and called us forth, convoking us to existence. He *"first* chooses man, in the eternal and consubstantial Son, to partake of divine filiation, and only *then* does he will the world's creation."[7]

---

[3] See Tertullian, *On the Resurrection*, 63.

[4] Each man "is included in the mystery of redemption, with each has Christ for ever united himself. . . . Each man comes into the world conceived in his mother's womb who then gives him birth. It is precisely by virtue of the mystery of redemption that man is entrusted to the solicitude of the Church. . . . The object of this solicitude is man in his unique and irrepeatable human reality, in which remains intact the image and likeness of God himself." John Paul II, *Redemptor hominis*, no. 13.

[5] *Christ Is Passing By*, no. 133.

[6] Ibid., no. 48.

[7] John Paul II, Audience, May 28, 1986, no. 4.

Through love God the Father created us to enjoy him without measure, wherein God delights. It is not possible for us to understand fully why he creates and loves us as if each alone walked the face of the earth. Yet this notion is central to humanity: "So we know and believe the love God has for us" (1 Jn 4: 16). Knowing and believing entail an intimate understanding born also of one's personal experience. If we can stretch our mind to glimpse God's plan, we do so only by virtue of the love God has planted in our hearts. "God has come to us, wretched creatures that we are, to tell us he loves us: 'My delight is to be among the sons of men' (Prov 8: 31). . . . No man is worthless to God. All of us are called to share in the heavenly kingdom, each with his own vocation: at home, at work, amid civic duties and exercising one's rights." [8]

Though our mind can barely grasp it, we can and ought to realize that we have been created "to enter into communion with God himself." [9] Can there be greater dignity?

## Prepared for divine union

In his goodness God has deigned to grant humanity the capacity to be drawn into his intimacy, making us *domestici Dei:* "members of the household of God" (Eph 2: 19). How easy it is for us to see God so, like a family! Therein our own experience prompts us to recognize how natural it is for each person to be infinitely loved. "Our God, in his most intimate mystery, is no solitude, but rather resembles a family, consisting of paternity, filiation, and the family's essence, Love subsistent." [10] Whereof any true love is but a mere reflection.

[8] *Christ Is Passing By*, no. 44.

[9] Ibid., no. 100.

[10] John Paul II, Homily, January 28, 1979. In his *Letter to Families* (February 2, 1994, no. 6), we read: "In light of the New Testament one can discover that the originating exemplar of the family is to be sought in God himself, in the Trinitarian mystery of his life. The divine 'we' represents the eternal model for the human 'we'; above all, for that 'we' is formed by man and woman, created in the divine image and likeness. The words of Genesis contain this truth about men, which furthermore agrees with humanity's very experience. Man is created 'in the beginning' as man and wife. The life of any human coalition, be it small or all-encompassing, is marked by this original duality. Whence are derived the

In this divine Family, amid Trinitarian life, humanity finds its home, thanks to God's most loving ways. To make this possible, God has endowed persons with a priceless dignity. Perhaps an example can shed light on the grandeur of our calling. Ordinarily no one is tempted to solder gold to some plastic piece. Not only is their value at opposite extremes, but the plastic would soon melt in the face of the soldering iron. Plastic is just not capable of being so joined to gold. Analogously we are to understand the quality possessed by our divinely wrought nature that enables us (though limitedly) to enter into communion with God himself. There we have "the great boldness of Christian faith: to proclaim the value and dignity of human nature and to affirm that we have been created to achieve the dignity of children of God through the grace that raises us up to a supernatural level. Incredibly bold it would be, were it not founded on the promise of salvation given to us by God the Father, confirmed by Christ's blood, and reaffirmed and made possible by the constant action of the Holy Spirit." [11]

## Introduced to God's intimacy

It is possible to achieve intimacy with God—the very life of the Father, the Son, and the Holy Spirit—by virtue of divine filiation. "Man's vocation, supreme indeed, is tied to divine filiation: our adoption as children in Christ, eternal Son, consubstantial with the Father." [12]

Men and women enter into the divine Family as children, partakers of God's life by virtue of being his children. And this takes place through the Father's only-begotten, the Word. Only he is Son. We are God's children by adoption, *through* the only-begotten. Therefore "the Church must be aware always of the dignity of divine filiation given to humanity in Christ, by grace of the Holy Spirit, and its destiny to grace and glory." [13]

The wonder of God's loving scheme for humans led Blessed

---

'masculinity' and 'femininity' of each person; whence also each community takes on its characteristic richness in the reciprocal complementarity of persons."

[11] *Christ Is Passing By*, no. 133.
[12] John Paul II, Homily, January 1, 1991.
[13] John Paul II, *Redemptor hominis*, no. 18.

*You Are a Child of God*

Josemaría to the brim of joy. "The knowledge that we have come from the hands of God, that the blessed Trinity looks upon us with favor, that we are children of so wonderful a Father," that is why "anyone who does not realize that he is a child of God is unaware of the deepest truth about himself. When he acts he lacks the dominion and self-mastery we find in those who love God above all else." [14] To recognize oneself as a child of God distinctively defines both one's being and one's role in the world, irrespective of circumstances. One's most intimate truth stems from divine filiation. This condition inspires every endeavor; it strengthens us in the face of hardship.

We have been created to take part in the intimacy of the holy Trinity; we are here on earth "to enter into communion with God himself. Jesus has promised us not a life of ease or worldly achievement but the house of his Father God, which awaits us at the end of the way (see Jn 14: 2)." [15]

Death will then be a homecoming: a return to the family home where God our Father awaits us. Filiation leads us to desire heaven. "How marvelous to hear our Father say, 'Well done, my good and faithful servant; because you have been faithful over a few things, I will set you over many; enter into the joy of your Lord' (Mt 25: 21)." [16] Everything in this life counts for little compared to what awaits us, but that little is to make us happy and win life eternal. If we act on the instinct of our divine filiation, while immersed in earthly affairs, we will also experience a thorough longing to find ourselves with God. Can one not desire to be with the person loved? Far from the end, death will be the beginning.

Dwelling on the amazing reality of divine filiation, our "words cannot go so far as the heart, which is moved by God's goodness. He says to us, 'You are my son.' Not a stranger, not a well-treated servant, not a friend—that would be a lot already. A son! He gives us free access to treat him as sons [would], with childlike piety, and I would even say with the boldness and daring of a child whose father cannot deny him anything." [17] Ours is to be the unlimited trust of a child with the best of parents.

[14] *Friends of God*, no. 26.
[15] *Christ Is Passing By*, no. 100.
[16] *Friends of God*, no. 221.
[17] *Christ Is Passing By*, no. 185.

How can our heavenly Father turn us down? True prayer is infallibly effective.[18] Unless we stop asking, Christ showed us, with clear and simple examples, that God hears our prayers and attends to them as a solicitous father. "[W]hat man of you, if his son asks him for bread, will give him a stone? Or if he asks for a fish will give him a serpent. . . . [H]ow much more will your Father who is in heaven give good things to those who ask him" (Mt 7: 9–11)! How pleased is God when we approach him as needy children.

## Sin costs us grace

Unfortunately humanity misused its high endowments. At history's dawn Adam fell from grace, and through him sin entered the world (see Rom 5: 12). "The story is as old as mankind. It began with the fall of our first parents; then came the unending depravities that punctuate the behavior of mankind through the ages; and finally, our own personal rebellions. It is very difficult to realize just how perverse sin is and to understand what our faith tells us. We should remember that even in the human context the scale of an offense is frequently determined by the importance of the injured party: his social standing and qualities. But with sin man offends God, the creature repudiates his creator."[19]

How mysterious is God's unbounded love for his creatures; how mysterious also is sin (*mysterium iniquitatis*)[20] whereby we grieve God. God's intent to welcome humanity to Trinitarian intimacy ran afoul of sin. Before sin we were God's children, sharing as such in God's life through grace. After original sin, no longer a participant in God's nature, humanity was left estranged, bereft of divine intimacy.

Such is our sad "inheritance," aggravated by personal sins. Contrary to the divine will, our being his grace-wrought children is forfeited by sin (grace is a gift, a favor), whereby we forsake familiarity with God. Let us go a step farther. A rebellious

[18] See Thomas Aquinas, *Summa Theologiae*, 2-2, q. 83, a. 2.
[19] *Christ Is Passing By*, no. 95.
[20] See 2 Thess 2: 7; also John Paul II, *Reconciliatio et paenitentia*, no. 14.

child who leaves home does not stop being his parents' child. Since being someone's child is irreversible, one cannot forsake filiation. Yet sin closes the door on intimate familiarity; it amounts to alienation, because the nature of a child of God is one cleansed and raised by grace, making of us "partakers of the divine nature" (2 Pet 1: 4).

Something's "nature" is that which makes it what it is and not something else. Take a building, for example. As it falls into ruin, it becomes "denatured," changed from what it once was.

On the other hand, a child who hates and rejects his parents is still their child. Our relationship with God is somewhat different. Forfeiting the gift whereby we become God's children and therefore heirs to heaven implies true disorientation; we thereby renounce our favored childlike condition. Yet, as we know from the parable of the prodigal son, God always looks upon us as a loving father. "In any case, since the young man is his son, no amount of misbehavior can alienate or destroy that relationship." [21]

The sin so thoroughly described in that parable "consists in rebelling against God, or at least in forgetfulness of, or indifference toward, him and his love." [22] The son wants to maneuver outside the divine reach, emigrating far away from the paternal home. "But this flight from God brings with it a situation of thorough confusion as to one's identity, along with the bitter experience of impoverishment and desperation. The prodigal son, so says the parable, then began to suffer need and was obliged, though born free, to serve one of the dwellers of that far region." [23] Sin signifies "the drama of lost dignity, the awareness of renouncing divine filiation." [24]

Souls close to God have well understood that a single sin— especially, but not just, a mortal one—constitutes a graver disorder than the worst cataclysm that could assail the earth. [25] To live as children of God, to dwell in divine intimacy, brings in its wake abhorrence for sin, even venial.

[21] John Paul II, *Dives in misericordia*, no. 5.
[22] John Paul II, Homily, September 17, 1989.
[23] Ibid.
[24] *Dives in misericordia*, no. 5.
[25] So affirms Cardinal J. H. Newman in *Apologia pro vita sua*.

# God's irrevocable fatherhood

However evil sin is, God still remains our Father, a Father, moreover, "rich in mercy" (Eph 2: 4). In his Gospel (15: 1–32), St. Luke regales us with parables of God's compassion for sinners and of his rejoicing over the recovery of a son who was lost. God the Father uses every possible means to restore persons ravaged by sin. He is the shepherd seeking his lost sheep, and when he finds it, he hoists it to his shoulders, acknowledging its fatigue and wounds. He is likened to a woman who, having lost a coin, lights a lamp, sweeps the house, and conscientiously searches until spotting it. He is the father, made impatient by love, who every day scans the horizon for his wayward son, hoping to make him out in every distant figure. . . . "In his great love for humanity," writes Clement of Alexandria, "God goes after man, much like the mother protectively hovers over a recently hatched bird fallen from its nest. And if it falls into the clutches of a serpent, the mother flutters about in sorrow for its loss. Thus, like a father, does God seek out his creature, curing it of its fall, pursuing the serpent till it relinquishes its prey, encouraging it to return, to fly back to the nest." [26]

"I tell you, there is joy before the angels of God over one sinner who repents" (Lk 15: 10). How can we keep our distance from confession if God takes such delight? How can we fail to bring our friends to the sacrament of mercy, wherein peace and joy and dignity are ours for the asking? God's merciful and paternal welcome will always be a powerful reason to repent. Before we can even raise our hand in search of help, God has already extended his to raise us up and help us go forward.

# Dignity regained

God the Father's love for his children was made manifest through the redemption. "The God of our faith is not a distant being who contemplates indifferently the fate of humanity: their desires, their struggles, their sufferings." [27] When the prodi-

---

[26] *Protrepticon*, GCS 12:10.
[27] *Christ Is Passing By*, no. 84.

gal son decides to return to the paternal farm to work as just another hired hand, his father, poignantly stirred by the son's sorry state, runs to meet him and lavishes him with every token of his love. "His father . . . ran and embraced him and kissed him" (Lk 15: 20). In an instant the prodigal son is restored to his sonship. "That's what the sacred text says: he covered him with kisses. Can you put it more humanly than that? Can you describe more graphically the paternal love of God for humanity?

"When God runs toward us, we cannot keep silent, but with St. Paul we exclaim, *Abba, Pater,* 'Father, my Father' (Rom 8: 15). Though he is the creator of the universe, he doesn't mind our not using high-sounding titles, nor worry about our not acknowledging his greatness. He wants us to call him Father; he wants us to savor that word, our souls filling with joy."[28] Accordingly we Christians have called him so often.

The father receives the son unconditionally, bidding him to forget the past. . . . His every thought is on the future, when restoring to him the dignity of faithful son. "The father said to his servants, 'Bring quickly the best robe, and put it on him; and put a ring on his hand, and shoes on his feet; and bring the fatted calf and kill it, and let us eat and make merry; for this my son was dead, and is alive again; he was lost, and is found'" (Lk 15: 22–24).

God's fatherly heart reaches down to any prodigal child, to any source of misery, especially our wretchedness. Then the object of all this divine compassion "does not feel humiliated, but renewed and again prized."[29]

In confession, by means of the priest, God restores in us whatever we culpably lost: both the grace and the dignity of children of God. Christ instituted this sacrament to spur our returning time and again to the paternal home. He fills us with grace and, if there is true contrition, he raises us up higher than we had been. Our Father God "draws, from our wretchedness, treasure; from our weakness, strength."[30] We go from being

[28] Ibid., no. 64.

[29] John Paul II, *Dives in misericordia,* no. 6.

[30] *Friends of God,* no. 309. "Our heavenly Father pardons any offense when his child returns to him, when he repents and asks for pardon. Our Lord is such a good father that he anticipates our desire to be pardoned and comes forward to us, opening his arms laden with grace." *Christ Is Passing By,* no. 64.

estranged children ("I am no longer worthy to be called your son," says the prodigal) to being good children again.

God's love impels us never to lose hope. He calls us to gratitude, to love, even when we have let ourselves be led by our weaknesses. By nature we are born only once, but in God's household, so rich in mercy, we are restored to full filiation as many times as we return repentant.[31]

## Children of God called to be saints

Thanks to Christ, we are again made capable of taking part in the Trinity's intimacy. Aptitude, capability, and potentiality are terms that speak to us of a possibility that only remotely existed before. But can we really be God's children? Only Christ is God's Son by nature: the only-begotten of the Father. Nonetheless, we can receive divine filiation, if we are admitted to, inserted into, Christ. We are, in him, children of the same Father. God has endowed us with sanctifying grace, which transforms us into another Christ, indeed Christ himself. The struggle to be holy in no way differs from the full effort to live divine filiation, to be each day better children of God.

What is involved? To love God and let oneself be loved by him, which is another way of saying to please God, to accomplish his will in everything. Now we "belong to Christ's family, for 'he himself has chosen us before the foundation of the world, to be saints, to be blameless in his sight, for love of him, having predestined us to be his adopted children through Jesus

---

[31] Thus does humility grow, giving rise to love for God. We discover that for our Father God, if we struggle, even our erring is converted into a reason for greater love. "Which of you . . . does not remember the arms of his father? They probably weren't as caressing, as gentle and tender as those of his mother. But our fathers' strong and powerful arms held us tight and safe and warm. Lord, I thank you for those tough arms. Thank you for those strong hands. Thank you for that sturdy and tender heart. I was going to thank you also for my errors! No, you don't want them! But you understand them, and excuse and forgive them.

"This is the wisdom God wants us to practice in our dealings with him. This indeed is a good mathematical lesson to learn to recognize that we are really a zero, but that our Father God loves each of us just as we are; yes, indeed, just as we are!" *Friends of God*, no. 148.

Christ, according to the purpose of his will' (Eph 1: 4–5). We have been chosen gratuitously by our Lord. His choice of us sets us a clear goal. Our goal is personal sanctity, as St. Paul insistently reminds us: *haec est voluntas Dei: sanctificatio vestra* ('this is the will of God, your sanctification'; 1 Thess 4: 3)."[32]

God calls each of us to strive to be holy, amid the circumstances around us. To that end, "he has in a certain way united himself with each of us."[33] His grace-effective call should head off any rationalizations behind which souls can take refuge in refusing to aim high. God's good children must be aware of the danger of conditioning the quest for holiness upon external situations of work, health, family, colleagues. . . . It is easy to fall into the temptation of finding excuses for not becoming God's friends in the very circumstances that should lead us to holiness. "Since I'm sick, now I can't think of committing myself to becoming a saint." "Since I have a sick child and many other occupations, I can't struggle to be close to God." "Since this is the exam season . . ." On the contrary, virtues grow and become solid thanks to adverse circumstances, even those very hard to bear. Often such straits represent the opportunity to recommit oneself to a deeper sanctity, to seek God with a purer intention, to find deeper meaning in the cross. . . .

Only in holiness do we find happiness. The holier, the happier.

---

[32] *Friends of God*, no. 2.
[33] Vatican II, *Gaudium et spes*, no. 22.2.

# CHAPTER 2

# Welcomed to God's Family
# As Children

## Divine filiation: true, thorough transformation

Earlier we noted that God makes us members of his family in a very particular way: through filiation. To call ourselves God's children is no euphemism. It is not just a compliment God pays to his creatures, like a mother calling her daughter "princess." God calls things by what they are; he calls us *children,* because in fact we are just that. Note how clearly and forcefully St. John speaks, " 'See how greatly the Father has loved us, that we should be counted as God's children; and so we are' (1 Jn 3: 1). God's children, siblings of the Word made flesh, kin of whom it was said, 'In him was life, and the life was the light of men' (Jn 1: 4). Children of the light, brothers of the light: that is what we are." [1] This fact colors our personality, the dignity marking our lives wherever we are found.

Divine filiation is a reality God has bestowed on humanity, a strictly supernatural dignity. He truly and really transforms us into his children. Thus should we understand St. John's amazement, "See how greatly the Father has loved us. . . ."

When we claim to be God's son or daughter, we do not indulge in some pious fantasy. We *are* his children. If human reproduction gives rise to "paternity" and "filiation," in a similar way those "engendered by God" are his children. This astounding reality begins with baptism, wherein a new life is born, one that did not exist before. Brought forth is "a new creature" (2 Cor 5: 17), which explains why the newly baptized is called and truly is a "child of God." Divine filiation is fundamental to a Christian's life—so understood and taught Blessed Josemaría Escrivá.

---

[1] *Christ Is Passing By,* no. 66.

*Natural* divine filiation takes place uniquely and eminently with the Son of God: "Jesus Christ, only-begotten Son of God, born of the Father before all ages . . . begotten, not made, consubstantial with the Father."[2] To distinguish between the Son's eternal filiation and our own, ours came to be called "adoptive." Here too we must be careful, lest divine adoption be reduced to earthly, wherein life is not transmitted, but only the parental name, rights to inherit, and the like. We are God's children because God's life fills our graced soul (see 2 Pet 1: 4). In giving us this filiation, "Christ not only assumed our nature, but also, in a weak, mortal body subject to suffering, he has become our blood brother. Because if the Word 'emptied himself, taking the form of a servant' (Phil 2: 7), he did so to make his brethren according to the flesh partake of the divine nature (see 2 Pet 1: 4). He does so in our earthly exile by means of sanctifying grace and in our heavenly homeland by eternal bliss."[3]

The fact that God is more our Father than those who gave us life should be a source of strength and help for us. When we call a Christian God's child, we are not merely employing an image of God's paternal vigilance over, and protection of, him or her. Rather, we are to understand it in its strictest sense, certainly more than when we say that so-and-so is a child of a particular couple.

We come to be by means of generation. Just as animals engender their kind of the same species, so too does humanity. Often the similarities are striking, and people are pleased to note the child's resemblance to his parents' features, build, ways of acting and speaking. . . . A Christian, then, born of God and truly his child, should resemble his or her heavenly Father. We are "partakers of the divine nature," in the words of St. Peter, implying more than an analogy, more than a resemblance or kinship. A Christian dwells in God's world.

The Word is the only Son of God. "A text of Jeremiah (3: 19) speaks of God's waiting to be invoked as Father: 'And I thought you would call me, My Father.' It is like a prophecy to be fulfilled in messianic times. Jesus of Nazareth more than fulfilled it in speaking of himself in relation to God as the one who

[2] Council of Nicea, Denz-Sch, 125.
[3] Pius XII, *Mystici Corporis*, no. 20.

'knows the Father,' for which he uses the sonlike expression *Abba*. The Father is always on Jesus' lips; he invokes the Father as one fully entitled to call upon him simply as '*Abba*—Father of mine.'"[4] A graced person enters into divine intimacy by partaking of the Son's filiation.

Behold a novelty. Man is called to participate in divine life, of that Life originating in the eternal processions of the most holy Trinity. It is that rebirth of which Christ spoke in intimate confidence to Nicodemus (see Jn 3: 3).

The certainty that God as a true Father desires the very best for his own should lead to entrusting ourselves to him serenely and joyfully, even in life's most troubled times. When a child of God comes across a hardship or setback, what is more natural than to ask his heavenly Father for more help and renew the effort to resemble him in that very setting?

---

[4] John Paul II, Address, July 1, 1987. He adds: "There's possibly no word that better expresses the self-revelation of God in the Son than '*Abba*—Father.' *Abba* is an Aramaic term, found in the Greek text of the Gospel of St. Mark (14:36). Jesus uses it in speaking to the Father. While the expression can be translated into any language, nonetheless, its coming from Jesus' lips allows us to glimpse its unique, unrepeatable content.

"In effect, *Abba* conveys the traditional praise of God: 'I thank you, Father, Lord of heaven and earth' (Mt 11:25). But it likewise reveals, when used by Christ, awareness of the unique and exclusive relationship between the Father and him, and him to the Father. It expresses the same reality to which Jesus alludes so simply yet extraordinarily in the text of Matthew's Gospel (11:27) and in that of Luke (10:22): 'No one knows who the Son is except the Father, or who the Father is except the Son and any to whom the Son chooses to reveal him.' That is to say, *Abba* manifests not only the mystery of the reciprocal links between Father and Son, but also synthesizes in some way all the truth of God's intimate life in its Trinitarian depths: the reciprocal knowledge of the Father and the Son whence emanates Love eternal.

"The word *Abba* forms part of the family's language and witnesses to the particular communion of persons that exists between a parent and the child he or she has engendered, between the child who loves his father and is loved by him. When Jesus used this word in speaking of God, it must have left its hearers amazed and even scandalized. An Israelite would never use it when praying. Only someone who saw himself as God's Son strictly speaking could speak thus of the Father and call upon him as Father. *Abba* means *my father, dad, daddy*."

# Divine filiation and humility

How wonderful it is to become members of God's family *in* and *through* the Son. It is simultaneously a gift and a mission to be carried out on earth. It is a divine gift, for whose growth we are ever to beg. Yet we are also to ready ourselves to receive it, since it is not something conquered by strong will, but by a flowering of grace, which best nestles in a humble soul. "No one knows . . . who the Father is except the Son and any to whom the Son chooses to reveal him" (Mt 11: 27).

Recognizing our littleness is the threshold by which we partake of God, engodden ourselves, since "humility means looking at ourselves as we really are, honestly and without excuses. And when we realize that we are worth hardly anything, we can then open ourselves to God's greatness: it is there our greatness lies." [5] Moreover, "it is our own wretchedness that leads us to seek refuge in God, to become Godlike. With him we can do all things." [6] As we experience our weakness and frailty, we seek out our heavenly Father for protection and warmth.

By extending divine adoption to us, "Jesus does not mind lowering himself in order to raise us from our destitution to the dignity of being children of God and brothers of his." [7] God's grandeur and the marvelous embrace he calls us to can be eclipsed by experiencing our waywardness, the flimsy stuff we are made of. But God already knows, and that did not stop him from choosing us. "Don't be afraid to know your real self. That's right, you are made of clay. Don't be worried. For you and I are children of God—and that is the right way of being made divine. We are chosen by a divine calling from all eternity: 'The Father chose us in Christ before the foundation of the world, that we should be holy and blameless before him' (Eph 1: 4). We belong especially to God, we are his instruments in spite of our great personal shortcomings. And we will be effective if we do not lose this awareness of our own weakness. Our temptations give us the measure of our own weakness." [8]

[5] *Friends of God*, no. 96.
[6] *The Forge*, no. 212.
[7] *Friends of God*, no. 112.
[8] *Christ Is Passing By*, no. 160.

A proud person "is always vainly striving to dethrone God ... so as to make room for himself and his ever cruel ways."[9] Such a person ends up in an evil godliness, worlds apart from the dignity arising from sharing in divine life. Such deception can lead to seeing oneself as "the sun and center of all those around him. Everything must revolve around himself."[10] Of such is the idolatry whereby a creature worships dust.

We have been saying that this childlike sharing in God, our godliness, is a divine gift. God graces us so we can receive it. Thus, he wants us "to empty ourselves, so that he can fill us. He wants us not to put obstacles in his way so that, humanly speaking, there will be more room for his grace in our poor hearts."[11] And the reason is that God wants to fill us with himself! So wrote St. Augustine: "For a vessel to be filled, it must first be empty. Cast therefore away from you all evil, for you are to be filled to the brim. Let's suppose that God wanted to fill you with honey. But if you're full of vinegar, where can the honey go? First we're to empty the vessel, washing and cleansing it, even if this requires effort, maybe even scrubbing, to make it ready to receive something."[12] Just as honey cannot fit in a vessel full of vinegar, neither can much honey be accommodated in a small vessel, however clean. Humility enhances and cleanses the heart. God fills the soul with divine filiation, but only to the degree that humility has emptied it, with the help of his grace.

What are we to do? Can we do less than seeking to please God, giving him all the glory, purifying our intention as often as necessary?[13] In view of such correspondence, "the infinite mercy of our Lord is not slow in coming to the aid of those who humbly call upon him. And then he acts as he truly is, as God Almighty."[14] Ours is a God whose power is as broad as his

---

[9] *Friends of God*, no. 100.

[10] Ibid., no. 101.

[11] Ibid., no. 98.

[12] *Commentary to the First Epistle of St. John*, 4, 2, 6.

[13] When we truly seek only to do God's will, we "are dealing a mortal blow to the selfishness and vanity that lurk in every conscience. At the same time, we will find true peace of soul through this selfless conduct that leads to an ever more intimate and intense possession of God." *Friends of God*, no. 114.

[14] Ibid., no. 104.

desire, and he desires nothing more than our being his children. Thus do personal humility and trust in God go hand in hand.

Children of God put their hope in their heavenly Father. Knowing and accepting their defects, they do not trust their own powers. They know enough to deploy all human means at hand, but above all they put their trust in prayer. They joyfully recognize and accept, moreover, that everything they have comes from their Father God. Humility consists not so much in self-loathing as in self-forgetfulness and effective concern for others. How could God despise anything divinely wrought? Interior simplicity leads us to experiencing the strength of God's children. "When everything seems to be collapsing before our eyes, we realize that quite the opposite is true, 'because you, Lord, are my strength' (Ps 43: 2). If God is dwelling in our soul, everything else, however important it may seem, is accidental and transitory, whereas we, in God, stand permanent and firm." [15]

## Sanctifying grace: participating in God's nature

St. John presents Christ as one "full of grace and truth" (1: 14); then he adds, "From his fullness we have all received, grace upon grace" (1: 16). Christ's soul is replete with grace; it is from that superabundance we receive grace, according to his will and our correspondence. Analogously to how God gives being to creatures, Christ, through his humanity, infuses grace in us. The Word's humanity is not only holy but also sanctifying, for through his holiness are humans hallowed.

At this point let us speak further of the godliness of children of God wrought by grace. When we say participating in God's nature, we are not, so to say, drawing something of God out of the Godhead—rather the opposite. God introduces creatures into himself. That is why the action is supernatural: welcoming created nature to his divinity, leaving us engoddened. Sacred Scripture (Ps 82) says, "You are gods." God's word is carried out in this case by our participating in the divine nature by means of grace.

---

[15] Ibid., no. 92.

Sanctifying grace cleanses human nature of sin, while raising it to God's level, so to speak. Evoking an earlier image, we can say that the honey that is grace cleanses, restores, and enhances the vessel that is our soul.

Grace elevates human nature, making us able to act as God's children, other Christs. It is like a new birth (see Jn 3: 3), which bestows on us new life, supernatural life, intended to grow and develop, so that with St. Paul we can say: "It is no longer I who live, but Christ who lives in me" (Gal 2: 20).

A human creature truly receives something beyond it, while remaining man or woman. It partakes of God's nature, a reception that is real but, as the philosophers say, "accidental." That means we continue to be what we were and will always be—a human cleansed and raised. Then, with the Apostle, we become a "new creature" (2 Cor 5: 17).

Our human personality is not lost or diminished by grace. Rather, it is lifted and transformed thanks to a new supernatural quality. It is somewhat similar to how steel exposed to heat, while remaining steel with all its metallic features, turns incandescent, with new characteristics, owing to the fire. Human nature supports the new supernatural personality of a child of God acquired through grace. Everything human is assumed and heightened by this divine influx.

This participating brings in its wake a closer similarity to God. To say that we partake of God the Son is to affirm that we participate in his sonship. Nevertheless, this does not mean that we partake solely of the Son. We take part in the one nature of the triune God. That grace-wrought access takes place, as we know, through the Son. It is therefore by and in the Son that we are introduced into God one and three.

We can therefore speak of a proper and particular relationship with the Son, with Christ. "Nothing can partake of something else except by means of what the latter is by its very nature," says St. Thomas Aquinas.[16] He goes on to say that "the adoption of children must necessarily be carried out by the natural Son." God the Son, in becoming man, has shown us the maximum a creature can aspire to in its closeness to God. It is an ideal we will never reach, for Jesus' human nature has been fully deified

---

[16] *Commentary on the Epistle to the Romans*, no. 48.

in its being assumed by the person of God's Son. In Christ "the whole fullness of deity dwells bodily" (Col 2: 9).

Christ fully and properly possesses what we receive partially and derivatively. His holy humanity is the instrument chosen by the Trinity to redeem and elevate humanity, making it possible for us to become intimate with God. With this free divine decision, mankind's natural dignity is elevated incomparably. If sin destroyed this marvel, redemption restores it even more admirably, leading us to participate even more closely in the Word's divine sonship.

The mystery of our being God's children is further enriched by our noting a fundamental Christian reality: the more one lives as God's child, the greater is our similarity and identification with Jesus. From this deepest of truths is born the desire to imitate Christ: divine filiation spurs us to emulate the words and deeds of the only-begotten Son. Blessed Josemaría exclaimed: "Lord, help me decide to tear off, through penance, this pitiful mask I have fashioned with my wretched doings. . . . Then, and only then, by following the path of contemplation and atonement, will my life begin to copy faithfully the features of your life. We will find ourselves becoming more and more like you. We will be other Christs, the Christ himself: *ipse Christus*." [17]

## Divine filiation: direction in our lives

"You are my son, today I have begotten you." These words from the second Psalm (v. 7) make reference above all to Christ, but they are applicable also to us. They can orient our entire day and life, however many our weaknesses, if we are committed to follow Jesus in the circumstances proper to each of us.

To be and behave as children of God, Blessed Escrivá emphasized, is not just one facet of our life. It defines who we are and determines how we are to relate to each event. Far from being just a particular virtue, just an aspect of Christian living, divine filiation is *the* fundamental status of a graced Christian. It pervades every virtue. Above and overall, we are children of God, in each circumstance, in every situation. This ironclad

[17] Josemaría Escrivá, *The Way of the Cross*, sixth station.

conviction ought to fill our living and doing. "We are children of God all day long," wrote Blessed Escrivá, "even though we do set aside special moments for considering it, so that we can fill ourselves with the awareness of our divine filiation, which is the essence of true piety." [18]

If we often consider the truth that "I'm God's child," we will resolutely find support in our Father God, on whom everything depends, especially when visited by troubles and adversities. We will more readily return to our Father's house, like the prodigal son. Prayer will become the trusting conversation of a child with his father, who understands and heeds his needy children. We will talk to God about what occupies our life: "everything that is on our mind and in our heart: our joys, sorrows, hopes, annoyances, successes, failures, even the most trivial happenings in our day. We will discover that our heavenly Father is interested in everything about us." [19]

When we live as God's good children, we see even the smallest activities of a routine day in the light of faith. It becomes customary for us to think and act in keeping with Christ's will. In the first place, we try to see all those we deal with as brothers and sisters, for we are all children of the same Father. Appreciating and respecting them will germinate the same desire filling Christ's heart: their holiness. Fraternal love will spur us above all to draw them ever more to God by their becoming more fully his children. Ours will reflect Christ's apostolic zeal for all.

A child is also heir, "entitled" to his father's goods: "heirs of God and fellow heirs with Christ" (Rom 8: 17). The second Psalm, a hymn to Christ's realm and divine filiation, continues: "Ask of me, and I will make the nations your heritage, and the ends of the earth your possessions." A foretaste of the promised heritage is ours already in this life: *gaudium cum pace,* the joy of knowing we are God's children is born of the union with God—not owing to our merits or health or success or easy sailing. It is grounded in knowing that God loves, embraces, and pardons us always . . . and has readied for us a place in heaven next to him for all eternity. This joy vanishes when we push aside the instinct of divine filiation and close our eyes to God's

[18] *Conversations with Monsignor Escrivá de Balaguer,* no. 102.
[19] *Friends of God,* no. 245.

will, ever wise and loving, behind the trials and strains each day brings.

Far be it for God to will our loss of joy. Like earthly parents (though much more so), he wants to see us happy always. Despite hardships, with this serene, cheerful attitude toward life (Blessed Josemaría liked to call it *gaudium cum pace* [20]), a Christian spreads much goodness on all sides. True joy is a powerful apostolic magnet.

---

[20] *Roman Missal*, preparation for Mass: *formula intentionis.*

# CHAPTER 3

# God's Children in Christ

## God's only Son: Jesus Christ

During his public life Jesus often referred to God's fatherhood with respect to humanity, evoking many expressions from the Old Testament. Nonetheless, "for Jesus, God is not merely 'the Father of Israel, the Father of men,' but rather *my Father. Mine*—this is the very reason why the Jews sought to kill Jesus, for he 'called God his Father' (Jn 5: 18). *Mine* is used in a completely literal sense: he whom the Son alone knows as Father and by whom the Son is uniquely and reciprocally known. . . . *My Father* is Jesus Christ's Father, the very origin of his being, mission, teaching."[1] Again, we are God's children by participating in Christ's sonship.

Near Caesarea Philippi, Simon Peter proclaims, "You are the Christ, the Son of the living God." Jesus replies, "Blessed are you. . . . For flesh and blood has not revealed this to you, but my Father . . ." (Mt 16: 16–17). "No one knows the Son except the Father"; just as "no one knows the Father except the Son" (Mt 11: 27). Only the visible Son makes visible the invisible Father. "He who has seen me has seen the Father" (Jn 14: 9). The Father and the Son know each other in a unique way. Never has there been nor will there ever be a more perfect intimacy. It is the identification of knowing and loving implied by the unity of the divine nature. With these various expressions, Jesus is declaring his Godhead.

As a Son consubstantial with the Father, Jesus reveals who God the Father is in our regard and how in the divine goodness he grants us the gift of the Holy Spirit. This was the nucleus of his revelation to humanity: the mystery of the most holy Trinity,

---

[1] John Paul II, Address, October 16, 1985.

and with and in it the marvel of divine filiation. At the Last Supper, in the intimacy of the Cenacle, Jesus sums up his years of deepest dedication and self-revelation when he declares, "I have manifested your name to the men whom you gave me" (Jn 17: 6). To "manifest the name" is to show somebody's way of being, one's essence. The Master made known to us the intimacy of the Trinitarian mystery: the fatherhood of God the Father, always hovering over us, and the love of the Holy Spirit. Both in intimate dialogues and when addressing the crowds, Jesus gives God the title of Father countless times. He speaks at length of his goodness as Father: rewarding even the smallest deed; prizing the good we do, however inconspicuous (see Mt 6: 3–4, 17–18); blindly generous in raining his gifts down upon just and unjust alike (see Mt 5: 44–46); always solicitous in attending to our needs (see Mt 8). He is never distant from our life, just like a father tending to his small child on the verge of danger.

Therefore, it is the entire Trinity that welcomes humanity to its intimate life, uniting us to infinite Love (the Holy Spirit), the first and fundamental gift, by which man becomes, in the Son, a child of the Father. We were baptized in their respective names upon entering into communion with the most blessed Trinity. In a certain way heaven has been opened to each of us, so that we can enter the Father's house and learn of our divine filiation. "If you had true piety," writes St. Cyril of Jerusalem, "on you too would descend the Holy Spirit, and you should hear the Father's voice from on high: 'This is not my son, but now after baptism he has become mine.'"[2] Divine filiation is one of the great gifts we receive the day we are baptized. Speaking of this filiation, St. Paul addresses each baptized when he pronounces those blissful words: "You are no longer a slave but a son, and if a son an heir" (Gal 4: 7).

There is only one Son in God, but we are also seen by God as his genuine children. Behold a mystery we can never fully comprehend. God, then, is not only our maker (as is a painter of his painting); God is our Father, who in mysterious and supernatural ways makes us "partakers of the divine nature" (2 Pet 1: 4). To be God's children is no human achievement, not a human advance, but an ineffable gift we should dwell on often and be

---

[2] *Catechesis* 3, on Baptism.

grateful for, every day. So recommended Blessed Josemaría: "Call him 'Father' many times a day and tell him (alone in your heart) that you love him, that you adore him, that you feel proud and strong because you are his child." [3]

## Divine filiation and identification with Christ

Christ, God's Son by nature, is the measure and scale of our life. "To be holy is to be a good Christian, to resemble Christ. The more closely a person resembles Christ, the more Christian he is, the more he belongs to Christ, the holier he is." [4] Like a student before the teacher, like a child learning from his mother, so a Christian should be before Christ. A child learns to speak by listening to his mother, trying to echo her words. Similarly, by watching Jesus we learn to behave like him. Christian life is imitating the Master, for he became enfleshed so "that you should follow in his steps" (1 Pet 2: 21). With these words the Apostle exhorts the first Christians to imitate the Lord: "Have this mind among yourselves, which was in Christ Jesus" (Phil 2: 5). Jesus is the exemplary cause of all holiness, that is, of God the Father's love. Not only for his deeds, but by his intimate being, Jesus' way of acting is the external expression of his union with and love for the Father.

Our sanctity consists not so much in imitating Jesus externally but, rather, in modeling our most intimate being after that of Christ. St. Paul encouraged the Colossians (3: 9–10): "Put off the old nature with its practices and . . . put on the new nature." With this phrase, St. Paul may have been borrowing from the theater, where the actors wore a mask representing the person being portrayed. Mask and actor are two different things; so too are the actor and the person portrayed. When St. Paul says to put on Christ, he is not calling for a mere change of clothes. What counts is our identifying with Christ, that we let ourselves be pervaded by grace.

St. Paul often points out that a redeemed person's new existence is life *in Christ:* "Therefore, if any one is in Christ, he is a

---

[3] *Friends of God*, no. 150.
[4] *The Forge*, no. 10.

new creation" (2 Cor 5: 17; see 1 Cor 1: 30; Rom 6: 11; etc.). Speaking of himself he affirms, "I have been crucified with Christ; it is no longer I who live, but Christ who lives in me" (Gal 2: 20). He indicates that his existence is enlivened by a vital power stemming from identification with the Lord. "For to me to live is Christ" (Phil 1: 21). Jesus himself had foretold it: "In that day you will know that I am in my Father, and you in me, and I in you" (Jn 14: 20).

This living "in Christ" also entails refining our habits, eliminating defects and whatever separates us from our Lord's life. Above all, however, it means that our way of being before our peers, the way we relate to others and to challenges, comes to resemble more each day Christ's actions in similar situations. Then our life somehow becomes an extension of his, for God "predestined [us] to be conformed to the image of his Son" (Rom 8: 29). Saints we will be, if God the Father can say of us what he one day said of Jesus: "This is my beloved Son, with whom I am well pleased" (Mt 3: 17). Our holiness will consist, then, of being by grace what Christ was by nature: God's children.

To "put on Christ," to "live in Christ" entails seeing the world and all others with Jesus' eyes. Ours is to be an understanding, generous, merciful gaze. We are to listen with Christ's ears, addressing others with words that spell peace, words that, far from hurting, heal, even if we must get them to forsake a false peace. Putting on Christ also means learning to work as he did, to obey like him, to love with his most-loving heart. This is what the saints have done.

The requirement for holiness in each of us, however different, is to resemble Christ. "You were amazed that I should approve of the lack of uniformity in that apostolate in which you work. And I said to you: 'Unity and variety. You have to be different from one another, as the saints in heaven are different, each having his own personal and very special characteristics. But also, you have to be as identical as the saints, who would not be saints if each of them had not identified himself with Christ.' "[5]

We are the Father's children because we are at one with Christ, though still retaining our own personality. Thus when

[5] *The Way*, no. 947.

we address the Father, it is Christ who prays in us; when we abstain from something for his sake, it is Jesus behind this spirit of discipline. When we wish to draw others to the sacraments, our apostolic zeal is but a mere echo of Jesus' craving for souls. Thanks to divine benevolence, our toils and sufferings complete those Christ underwent for his Mystical Body, which is the Church. How invaluable then become the work, pain, trials of unsensational days. In a way our life is a continuation of Jesus' earthly existence. He truly lives in us.

Blessed Josemaría at times addressed those in his company: "I see coursing within you Christ's very blood." He recognized the firm efforts of those at his side to identify themselves with the Master, an identification that somehow was reflected in their gaze, face, deeds. This was no idle phrase. Antonio Aranda remarks that the energy with which he said them was moving: "He said them with great conviction and no less joy. With the simplicity of spontaneous words expressed with the lips, eyes, heart, his attitude was that of someone manifesting a deep certainty that stirred and captivated him. That telling reference to Christ's blood, his life, enlivening Christians at their core also illuminated the spirit of dedication and service to everyone amid ordinary life that Blessed Josemaría sought to pass on. But above all, though some of us did not then fully realize it, it principally was a glimpse of his interior gaze, of his loving contemplation of Christ's mystery."[6] He looked upon others through Christ, with Christ's gaze.


## Growth in holiness

"God shows to men, in a vivid way, his presence and his face in the lives of those companions of ours in the human condition who are more perfectly transformed into the image of Christ (cf. 2 Cor 3: 18)."[7] Such union with God is so alive in a saint that one can perceive in him, almost tangibly, God's personal presence. In his saints' gestures, words, and fellowship, it is Christ himself who, in a way, shows himself. Whatever one's

---

[6] Antonio Aranda, *Scripta Theologica*, 26:517.
[7] Vatican II, *Lumen gentium*, no. 50.

character, upbringing, environment, cultural legacy, and vital experiences, each saint reveals the image of Jesus Christ. The experience of divine things, found in various moments of life, enriches our faith, spurs us onward, and draws Christ closer to us. Have we not all seen how in families the children, without realizing it, imitate their parents: pick up their gestures and mannerisms, even how their parents think and act?

"Well, the same kind of thing happens to a good child of God. One finds oneself acquiring—without knowing how, or by what means—a marvelous godliness, which enables us to focus on events from the supernatural viewpoint of faith; we come to love all people as our Father in heaven loves them and, what is more important, we become more fervent in our daily efforts to come closer to God." [8]

Holiness is God at work in our souls through grace. It is a new, acquired way of being. God's life comes our way through grace, which "renews man from within and converts a sinner and rebel into a good and faithful servant (see Mt 25: 21). The source of all grace is God's love for us, and he has revealed this not just in words but also in deeds." [9] Imitating Christ's gestures, deeds, virtues, his essence, is the goal we are to reach for. In a way Jesus wants to continue living in us, to keep on working and redeeming through us. A Christian is Jesus' limb (see 1 Cor 12: 27). Our transformation is through the work of the Holy Spirit, who in sculpting Christ in our souls drives home to us the joyful and ineffable reality of our filiation to God the Father.

On this path to holiness God asks us to take one step after another, however slight, beginning anew each time we stumble. He does not expect superhuman feats from us, but rather supernatural acts that are within our reach, thanks to grace. On this journey, "Christ, united to the Father and to every person, continually sends the Spirit, who in turn infuses in us the sentiments of the Son and directs us to the Father." [10]

---

[8] *Friends of God*, no. 146.
[9] *Christ Is Passing By*, no. 162.
[10] John Paul II, *Redemptor hominis*, no. 18

# Like little children: spiritual childhood

God expects us to behave in keeping with what we are: weak, young children ever in need of his help. We should live like children, always trusting in their heavenly Father. Though not every saint has done so explicitly, a dependent attitude characterizes them all, for the Holy Spirit brings it about. He inspires in us a pure heart typical of innocent children, even when faced with pain and hardship. "A foolish child wails and stamps his feet when his loving mother puts a needle to his finger to get a splinter out. A sensible child, on the other hand, perhaps with his eyes full of tears—for the flesh is weak—looks gratefully at his good mother who is making him suffer a little in order to avoid much greater harm. Jesus, may I be a sensible child."[11]

We are to understand that behind sickness, professional setbacks, and the like is found the provident hand of the Father, who cannot stop watching out for his children. Spiritual childhood leads us to accept with a joyful and thankful heart whatever life has to offer, be it sweet or bitter, as something sent or permitted by One who is infinitely wise and could not love us more.

A life of spiritual childhood entails simplicity, humility, abandonment, but not immaturity. "A foolish child wails and stamps": *l'enfant terrible* is immature of mind, heart, and emotions; missing are self-discipline and moral struggle. Such an infantile attitude is compatible with any age; it stems from not seeing oneself as a true child of God. Authentic spiritual childhood betrays a mature mind: supernatural outlook, pondering events in the light of faith and aided by the Holy Spirit's gifts. Yet, given that, it is not any less simple or uncomplicated: "a sensible child . . . looks gratefully. . . ." Conversely, far from this life of childhood is the immature person, fickle with respect to desires, ideas, events, emotions, bobbing like a cork on the waves and trapped within his own ego. Yet a sensible child, weak but simple, is wholly out to glorify his Father God.

In Christian life maturity comes only when we make ourselves children before God, children of his who trust and abandon themselves in him, like a toddler in his father's arms. Then

[11] *The Forge*, no. 329.

we see earthly happenings for what they are, in their true value, and our only concern is to please our Father and Lord.

To become childlike (but not childish) is a spiritual path requiring the supernatural virtue of fortitude, lest we not overcome pride and self-sufficiency. Such hinder us from behaving as God's children and lead, when confronted with repeated failures, to discouragement, barrenness, and loneliness.

A Christian who sets out to live a spiritual childhood finds living charitably easier, because, as St. Maximus of Tours remarks, "a child is a creature bereft of resentment, unfamiliar with cheating and deceit. A Christian, like a small child, meets insult with equanimity... and doesn't seek revenge when treated badly. Even more: God demands of him to pray for his enemies, to give up his tunic and mantle to those in need, to turn the other cheek when buffeted" (see Mt 5: 40).[12] A child easily forgets and does not nurse wounds, he becomes in fact a relative stranger to suffering.

Spiritual childhood keeps its love always fresh, because simplicity soon dismisses from the heart negative experiences. "You've become younger! You notice, in fact, that getting to know God better has made you regain in a short time the simple and happy age of your youth, including the security and joy—without any childishness—of spiritual childhood. . . . You look around and realize that the same thing has happened to others. the years since they met up with God have gone by and, having reached maturity, they are strengthened with a permanent youth and happiness. Although they are no longer young, they are youthful and happy!

"This reality of interior life attracts, confirms, and wins over souls. Give thanks for it daily *ad Deum qui laetificat iuventutem,* to God who fills your youth with joy."[13] God truly rains down joy on the unending youth of the beginnings, middle years, and old age. God is always the greatest joy in life if we live as children before him, as tiny and ever needy creatures.

---

[12] *Homily,* 58.
[13] Josemaría Escrivá, *Furrow,* no. 79.

CHAPTER 4

# Stages of Identification
# with Christ

Blessed Josemaría Escrivá used to speak of four stages in identifying ourselves with Christ: to seek him, to find him, to get acquainted with him, and to love him. He further advised, "It may seem clear that you are only at the first stage. Seek him then, hungrily; seek him within yourselves with all your strength. If you act with determination, I am ready to guarantee that you have already found him, and have begun to get to know him and to love him, and to hold your conversation in heaven" (see Phil 3: 20).[1]

## Seeking Christ

*Overcoming obstacles*

To seek God we must first rebel against the enemies of our holiness. It will be a struggle; a Christian's is not an easy path. "Get used to saying *No*," advised Blessed Josemaría, as a means to rein in our caprices and thoughtlessness. We're to say *No* to laziness and apathy, to self-indulgence and comfort. The "law of sin," of which Paul speaks (Rom 7: 23), in many souls means the "law of whims or getting one's own way." It leads to "that disease of character whose symptoms are a general lack of seriousness, unsteadiness in action and speech, foolishness—in a word, frivolity."[2]

A frivolous person is inconstant, moody, dislikes standards and justifiable motives. By virtue of such uncertainty and light-

---

[1] *Friends of God*, no. 300.
[2] *The Way*, no. 17.

headedness, he can easily end up hollow, unprincipled—the very opposite of holiness. Saying *No* to many things permits saying *Yes* to what God is asking.

To bring about an uncluttered terrain favorable to the Holy Spirit, we should also be forewarned of the danger of reducing the faith to something merely emotional or sentimental. Such an attitude is all about feelings: "I feel the need"; "I'm eager"; "I don't feel like. . . ." This dependency blocks supernatural outlook, any movement to holiness. Under its unstable sway one's spirit soars with fleeting enthusiasm and plummets when hardship comes along. Following Christ then resembles nothing so much as fireworks, wherein heat and light are soon extinguished. A determined pledge to second God's will in everything is what alone can weather life's ups and downs.

A love for Christ that is ever stronger permits us to moderate our moods. We can then harness what is positive in them, while recognizing that sentiments, however important in dealing with God and in human affairs, cannot be the main reason for our endeavors. Sentiment can be a big help, but nothing more. It cannot set the pace or choose the destination.

## A loving struggle

To seek Christ each day is, in large measure, a question of making resolutions. These should be formulated and carried out by bringing to our interior struggle a sense of urgency, by focusing on achieving the goal in the short term. We also should count on heaven's help, knowing full well that any occasion can serve to draw us closer to God.

Let us never forget that God our Father saves and sanctifies us, and he is infinitely more committed to this objective than we are. He sends us whatever assistance we may need in addition to arranging circumstances to spur us to identify ourselves more and more with his Son. The awesome reality is that the "divine stake" in our holiness gives a particular "shape" to our efforts to improve. We bring to the interior struggle a trusting, filial attitude of abandonment to God's wishes and power. We need not "clench our teeth" as if victory depended solely on us. Each of us should be able to say: "I love the will of my God; that is why, abandoning myself completely into his hands, I pray that he may lead me however and wherever he likes."[3] Then let us busy ourselves with truly pleasing our Father.

A person who largely relies on his own strength and experience forgets that without God's help nothing is achieved: "Apart from me you can do nothing" (Jn 15: 5). We are to understand truly that the interior life rests, above all, in knowing that we are loved by God both paternally and exclusively, as if each of us were the only person in the world. "We know and believe the love God has for us," said the apostle St. John (1 Jn 4: 16), mindful of his days next to Jesus.

*God loves each of his children.* This consoling truth should preside over the soul's efforts to be better, to approach Jesus Christ. We always count on the love of God the Father, who, even in the worst moments of our existence, is always at work. However wrong and weak, we ought never to forget our Father's loving aid to return us to the good path. He sustains us in the fight.

Under the umbrella of this filial trust, we should also keep in mind that saints are not just those who never go astray, but those who seriously commit themselves to do the right thing, nevertheless fail, and then humbly repent. They rise optimistically to take up the struggle again. It is a question of beginning again, of pleasing[4] above all one's heavenly Father. Whoever loves seeks to please the beloved, at whatever personal sacrifice.

Ours cannot be a superhuman ascetical struggle to reach certain goals, much as we might strive to do in any other challenging endeavor. Rather we are to carry out supernatural deeds made feasible only by grace. God could not care less for "self-perfection"; he only desires to see us grow in love. That is why we should focus, not so much on the physical fulfillment of a given

---

[3] *The Forge,* no. 40.

[4] St. Teresa of Avila often speaks of giving the Lord pleasure, contentment, joys, satisfaction. "To love is seeking to please God in everything" (*Mansions,* 4.1, 7). "The will to please God and faith both make possible what is impossible to natural reason" (*Foundations,* 2.4). From the same work: "Self love . . . seeks to please ourselves more than God" (5.4); "God delights in our obedience more than in our sacrifices" (6.2). From *The Path to Perfection:* "This house is heaven . . . for whoever is content to make God content and ignores one's own contentment" (13.7); "What do kings and lords matter to me, if for their sake I should, even slightly, displease God?" (2.5).

virtue, as on the love for Christ invested in the struggle to achieve it. The object is not to end the fray with nary a misstep but to commit ourselves to fulfill lovingly God's will in everything.

Our Father God knows well the depths of the human heart and the wretchedness rooted there. He always understands and encourages us to keep up the struggle in every setting. He does not idealize us in his unbounded love for us, but rather sees us with our weaknesses and inconsistencies, capable of both good and evil. "He knows what's inside of man. Only he knows!"[5] Yet, despite everything, he asks us to set out: "Come, follow me" (Lk 18: 22).

The spiritual life of any saint is the story of the love of God, who so often looks on each with favor, who so often goes out to seek them. At times, however, more than a few who have not been completely faithful foolishly imagine that God has revoked his love. And the devil soon takes advantage of this untruth to lead souls astray, precisely when they are most in need of God. In such sorry straits they may receive more divine favors, as shown in the parables that particularly deal with divine mercy: the prodigal son, the lost sheep, the missing drachma [silver coin] that, once found, are cause for so much celebration.

Let us recall often that any moment is apt for trustingly beginning anew. Let us reject being overcome by the negative experiences of current frailties and past sins. Let us never think we are alone. Struggling against our failings to "make our Father happy," to behave as he wants, will spur us to acquire virtues.[6]

## Finding Christ

Truly, to seek Christ is, in a way, to have found him already. He arranges for us to cross his path, if only we seek him.[7]

[5] John Paul II, Address, October 22, 1978.

[6] See *The Forge*, no. 346.

[7] "Just think about the wonder of God's love. Our Lord comes out to meet us, he waits for us, he's by the roadside where we cannot but see him, and he calls each of us personally, speaking to us about our own things—which are also his. He stirs us to sorrow, opens our conscience to be generous; he encourages us to want to be faithful, so that we can be called his disciples." *Christ Is Passing By*, no. 59.

We find Jesus in the Gospel: there he speaks to us, there we see our model, there he instructs us. That is why, as did many saints, Blessed Josemaría advised us "to read books on the Lord's passion. Such works, full of true piety, bring to our minds the Son of God, a man like ourselves and also true God, who in his flesh loves and suffers to redeem the world." Then, if we try to imitate him, Jesus "is . . . reflected in our behavior, as in a mirror. If the mirror is as it ought to be, it will capture our Savior's most lovable face without distorting it or making a caricature of it; and then other people will have an opportunity of admiring him and following him." [8] In the holy Gospels we learn how to imitate him and follow his steps in being children of the Father. Then we want to identify ourselves with him, so that our life, amid our tasks, reflects his. [9]

One cannot love what is not familiar. That is why we must have Christ's life "in our heart and mind, so that at any time, without any book, we can close our eyes and contemplate his life, watching it like a movie. In this way the words and actions of our Lord will come to mind in all the different circumstances of our life.

"In this way we become involved in his life. It is not a matter of just thinking about Jesus, of recalling some scenes of his life. We must be completely involved and play a part. . . . If we want to bring other men and women to God, we must first go to the Gospel and contemplate Christ's love." [10]

We turn to the Gospels desirous of contemplating the Savior

---

[8] *Friends of God*, no. 299. On another occasion he said, "Make it a habit to mingle with the characters who appear in the New Testament. Capture the flavor of those moving scenes where the Master performs works that are both divine and human; he tells us, with human and divine touches, the wonderful story of his pardon for us and his enduring love for his children. Those foretastes of heaven are renewed today, for the Gospel is always true. . . ." Ibid., no. 216; see no. 222.

[9] "To be Christ himself, we must *see ourselves in him*. It's not enough to have a general idea of the spirit of Jesus' life; we have to learn the details of his life and, through them, his attitudes. And especially we must contemplate his life, to derive from it strength, light, serenity, peace.

"When you love someone, you want to know all about his life and character, so as to become like him. That is why we have to meditate on Jesus' life, from his birth in a stable right up to his death and resurrection." *Christ Is Passing By*, no. 107.

[10] Ibid.

as his disciples saw him, to observe their reactions, how they behaved, what they said . . . to see him overflow with mercy when
faced with so many needy people, tired after a long stretch of
walking, marveling at the faith of a mother or of the centurion,
patient in the face of his closest followers' shortcomings. . . . We
also contemplate how he deals habitually with his Father, the
trusting way he turns to him, those nights of prayer . . . his abid-
ing love for one and all.

## Finding Christ in the sacraments

We encounter Jesus in the sacraments, especially in penance and
the sacred Eucharist. In confession Christ is always willing to
give us again, if necessary, divine life and the instinct of divine
filiation. "If you should stray from him for any reason, react with
the humility that will lead you to begin again and again; to play
the role of the prodigal son every day, and even repeatedly during the twenty-four hours of the same day; to correct your contrite heart in confession, which is a real miracle of God's love. In
this wonderful sacrament our Lord cleanses your soul and fills
you with joy and strength to prevent you from giving up the
fight, and to help you keep returning to God unwearied, when
everything seems black." [11] Immediately, next to Christ in the
tabernacle, light returns. Our soul's pride "can be transformed
into humility. Then, true joy wells up in our hearts, even though
we feel that the wings of our souls are still clogged with mud,
the clay of our wretchedness that is now beginning to dry. If we
practice mortification, the mud will fall off, allowing us to soar
very high, because the wind of God's mercy will be blowing in
our favor." [12]

We find Jesus in the tabernacle; he could be only feet away.
Why don't we go to see him, to love him, to tell him our ideas,
to ask for his help? There the Master has been waiting for us for
twenty centuries.[13] Then we will be able to be next to him, like
Mary, Lazarus' sister who chose the better part for herself (see
Lk 10: 42), in their house in Bethany. Says Blessed Josemaría,

[11] *Friends of God*, no. 214.
[12] Ibid., no. 249.
[13] See *The Way*, no. 537.

"For me the tabernacle has always been a Bethany, a quiet and pleasant place where Christ resides. A place where we can tell him about our worries, our sufferings, our desires, our joys, with the same sort of simplicity and naturalness as Martha, Mary, and Lazarus. That's why I rejoice when I stumble upon a church in town or in the country; it's another tabernacle, another opportunity for the soul to escape and join in intention our Lord in the sacrament." [14]

When praying before the tabernacle we can say in all truth and reality: *God is here*. And faced with this mystery of faith we can but exclaim: *Adoro te devote* (Devoutly I adore you, O hidden God). Respect and amazement follow adoration, not to mention unwavering trust. "Remaining before Christ the Lord, the faithful enjoy his intimate acquaintance; they open their hearts asking for themselves and for theirs, while begging for the world's peace and salvation. Offering with Christ their whole lives to the Father in the Holy Spirit, they draw from this wonderful intimacy an increase of faith, hope, and charity." [15]

Being God's children, then, should give us a strong desire to get acquainted with Jesus in the tabernacle, to receive him intimately at communion. "I can understand your keenness to receive the holy Eucharist each day. Those who feel they are children of God have an overpowering need of Christ." [16]

## Becoming acquainted with Christ

"There is only one way to become more familiar with God, to increase our trust in him. We must come to know him through prayer; we must speak to him and show him, through a heart to heart conversation, that we love him." [17]

We Christians are not limited to a single, systematic way of praying. "We children of God don't need a method, an artificial system, to talk with our Father." [18] Our prayer ought to be as

[14] *Christ Is Passing By*, no. 154.
[15] Congregation for the Sacraments, *Instruction on the Eucharistic Mystery*, May 25, 1967, no. 50.
[16] *The Forge*, no. 830.
[17] *Friends of God*, no. 294.
[18] Ibid., no. 255.

spontaneous as that of a child speaking with a parent, of a friend with a friend. Each of us should find his own way of praying, according to his soul's needs at that particular stage in his life.[19]

Our prayer should resemble a fire feeding on our meditating on the Gospel and the truths of Christian faith.[20] Ours is the prayer of God's children: trusting, personal (not hiding behind anonymity), sincere, desirous always of fulfilling our heavenly Father's will.

At prayer we are with Jesus. Is that not enough? We pray to dedicate ourselves to him, to know him, and to learn how to love. The way we pray cannot be divorced from our current circumstances: our activities, the joys that come our way, the hardships . . . that turn into joy next to Christ. Often we will call to mind a Gospel passage to contemplate Jesus' most holy humanity and thus we learn to love him. Then we will see if we are truly sanctifying our work, if it leads us to God; or how we are getting along with those with whom we spend our life: family, friends. . . . Sometimes a sentence from a book we have been reading will spark a conversation. Or we will direct to God an aspiration that occurs to us; or we will dwell on an affection planted in our soul by the Holy Spirit. On other occasions we will draw up a small resolution to be carried out that day, or we will revive a previous one. . . .

[19] "What do lovers say when they meet? How do they behave? They sacrifice themselves and all their belongings for the person they love. First, one brief aspiration, then another, and another . . . till our fervor seems insufficient, because words are too poor . . . then this gives way to intimacy with God, looking at God without needing rest or feeling tired. We begin to live as captives, as prisoners. And while we carry out as perfectly as we can (with all our mistakes and limitations) the tasks allotted to us by our situation and duties, our soul longs to escape. It is drawn towards God like iron drawn by a magnet. One begins to love Jesus, in a more effective way, with the sweet and gentle surprise of his encounter." Ibid., no. 296. Thus what began as familiarity with Jesus' holy humanity is turned into an "insatiable hunger, an uncontrollable yearning to contemplate his face." *The Way of the Cross*, sixth station, no. 2.

[20] "Live your life close to Christ. You should be another character in the Gospel, side by side with Peter, and John, and Andrew. For Christ is also living *now: Iesus Christus, heri et hodie, ipse et in saecula!* Jesus Christ lives! Today, as yesterday, he is the same, for ever and ever." *The Forge*, no. 8.

Mental prayer is a task calling for our mind and will, aided by grace. We should be ready to reject distractions, never welcoming them voluntarily. We should strive to develop a dialogue with God, the essence of every prayer. Speak to him from the heart, gazing upon him, hearing his voice in the intimacy of your soul.

Next to Christ in the tabernacle (or wherever we pray mentally), we shall persevere out of love, whether joyful or straining amid apparent barrenness.[21] Often it is helpful to know that we are united to Christians praying the world over. Our voice adds itself to the clamor being raised at every moment to God the Father, through the Son, in the Holy Spirit.

By persevering in daily prayer we find the origin of our identification with Christ, the habitual source of our joy, provided we make an effort and go there determined to be "alone with who we know loves us."[22] Love for God progresses at the pace of our prayer and positively affects our actions, work, apostolate, mortification. . . .

Crucial to spiritual progress, the soul should be alert to the so-called "failure in prayer: discouragement during periods of dryness; sadness that, because we have 'great possessions' (Mk 10: 22), we have not given all to the Lord; disappointment over not being heard according to our own will. . . ."[23] We should promptly identify these "failures" in order to seek the proper remedy and to persevere in a filial relationship with God.

---

[21] One trouble, "especially for those who sincerely want to pray, is dryness. Dryness belongs to contemplative prayer when the heart is separated from God, with no taste for thoughts, memories, or feelings, even spiritual ones. This is the moment of sheer faith—clinging faithfully to Jesus in his agony and in his tomb. 'Unless a grain of wheat falls into the earth and dies it remains alone; but if it dies, it bears much fruit' (Jn 12:24). If dryness is due to the lack of roots, because the word has fallen on rocky soil, the battle requires conversion (see Lk 8:6, 13)." *Catechism of the Catholic Church*, no. 2731.

[22] St. Teresa of Avila, *Life*, 8.2.

[23] *Catechism of the Catholic Church*, no. 2728.

# Loving Christ

## God the Father asks for all

God does not ask merely for another place in his children's heart, soul, and mind, alongside other loves. Rather he seeks *all* our love, not a bit of attention or a tad of devotion. God seeks our entire being, without measure or end. He is a "jealous lover," begging for all our desire. He awaits our giving him all we have, following the personal vocation wherewith he called us one day and keeps on calling us every day amid the duties and circumstances, pleasant or less so, that befall us. "God has a right to ask us: Are you thinking of me? Are you aware of me? Do you look to me as your support? Do you seek me as the light of your life, as your shield . . . as your all?

"Renew, then, this resolution: In times the world calls good I will cry out: 'Lord!' In times it calls bad, again I will cry: 'Lord!' " [24] Each circumstance is a chance to love him whole-heartedly, with one's entire soul and existence, not only when we go to church to visit him or receive communion . . . but also in the thick of work, in the face of suffering and failure, when unexpected good news reaches us. Then, let us say to him in our soul's depths: "Father of mine, I love you, I will peaceably accept this annoyance for your sake, I will bring this chore to a full close, done just right, because I know it pleases you. . . ."

We are also bound to love our Father God with our heart of flesh, affectionately, with the only heart we possess. Both human and supernatural is the love we contemplate in God's Son. Jesus is full of warmth, interest, and tenderness when we turn to his heavenly Father and when he converses with us. He is moved by a widow mourning the loss of her only son; he cries over a friend who has died; he appreciates the gratefulness of lepers who have been cured; he is always cordial and open to all, even amid the excruciating yet sublime stages of his passion. . . . God's children need to remind themselves often that Christian life consists not "in much thinking, but in much loving." [25]

[24] *The Forge*, no. 506.
[25] St. Teresa of Avila, *Interior Castle*, 4:1, 7.

*Loving with a steadfast will*

Faced with emotions and sentiments, we often feel downtrod-
den and desire help and protection, kindness and happiness. . . .
And those moods, sometimes very deep, can and ought to be
the occasion to grow in the conviction of our divine filiation, to
tell our Father God that we sorely need his help. If our conduct
were only the result of dispassionate, rational choice (ignoring
thereby the affective side of our being), we would not be conducting ourselves fully as God wants. We might even end up not
loving him. God made us with body and soul, and with our
complete being—heart, mind, strength—the Master says we are
to love him.

It may happen that we are cold and reluctant, as if our heart
was frozen, because emotions come and go in unforeseen ways.
Disheartened, it may be difficult to follow our path feeling as if
we must fulfill an onerous duty or take a bitter medicine. We are
to use the means to leave that condition behind. Instead of a
passive purification sent by God, it could be proof of luke-
warmness, of scant true love. We are to love with a firm will and,
whenever possible, with the noble sentiments our heart con-
tains. With divine help, more often than not, we will be able to
awaken our affection, to set our heart ablaze, even in the absence
of interior satisfactions.

At other times God plays the role of a kindhearted mother,
who rewards her unsuspecting child with something sweet or
just wants to show her fondness for her little one. And the child,
who already loves her, turns gleeful and even volunteers to do
something to show his gratitude. And when the candies are not
forthcoming, the child does not conclude that maternal love has
disappeared; with additional common sense the child will see
her loving heart behind a correction or a visit to the doctor. So
will we with our Father God, who loves us infinitely more.
When consolations are present, let us take advantage of them to
draw closer to him, to correspond more generously in the daily
struggle, even though we realize that love's essence is not a
bunch of sentiments.

## Cultivating love

We are to protect and feed our love. We are to put our affectionate heart into our piety. We cannot expect to advance with just gritted teeth and a stoic attitude that all too soon cools and impoverishes our love for Christ. Let us never forget that in our dealings with God the heart is a valued ally. "Your mind is sluggish and won't work. You struggle to collect your thoughts in God's presence, but it's useless: a complete fog. Don't force yourself, and don't worry either. Listen closely: it is the hour for your heart." [26]

Perhaps then is the time to say to God a few simple words, as we did when we were younger, to repeat attentively some aspirations full of piety and fondness. Those who walk the paths of our loving God know well how important it is to use words, deeds, gestures that encompass love day after day.

To love God as dear children we are to turn often to the only-begotten Son's most holy humanity: contemplating him as perfect God and perfect man. Let us observe how he reacts to those who approach him: his mercy, compassion, love for all. Let us meditate on his Passion and death on the cross: his unbounded generosity when in the throes of supreme pain. At other times let us address God in the words that express human love. We can even convert popular songs of true love into genuine prayer; Blessed Josemaría did so often.

Loving God, like any authentic love, is not a mere sentiment or emotion unto itself. It should foster other loving relationships and act as the mainspring for our every endeavor.

## Self-sacrificing love

The more one develops in holiness, the more the cross appears as a fixture. "Do not forget that being with Jesus means we shall most certainly come upon his cross. When we abandon ourselves into God's hands, he frequently permits us to taste sorrow, loneliness, opposition. . . . This is the time to love passive mortification, which comes, hidden perhaps or barefaced and insolent, when we least expect it. . . . So does Jesus fashion the

---

[26] *The Way*, no. 102.

souls of those he loves, while never failing to give them inner calm and joy . . . and he impresses on them a living conviction that they will find comfort only when they make up their minds to do without it."[27] In suffering a soul discovers with heightened relief the reality of divine filiation. "God is my Father, though he sends me suffering. He loves me tenderly, even when hurting me. Jesus suffers to carry out the Father's will. . . . And I, who also want to fulfill God's most holy will, following in the Master's footsteps, can I complain when I find suffering along the way?

"That will be a sure sign of my filiation, because God treats me as he treated his own divine Son."[28] It is in the midst of ordinary life, on the street, in the home, with the family, immersed in our jobs, that we are to attain union with Christ, thereby becoming "another Christ."

Everything began with the quest for Christ. And now one can understand the serenity and joy with which he carries his cross. "When you walk where Christ walked; when you are no longer just resigned to the cross, but your whole soul takes on its form, takes on its very shape; when you love the will of God; when you actually love the cross . . . then, only then, is it he who carries it."[29]

[27] *Friends of God*, no. 301.
[28] *The Way of the Cross*, first station, no. 1.
[29] *The Forge*, no. 770.

# CHAPTER 5

# The Holy Spirit and Divine Filiation

## The Paraclete's mission

The Gospels often refer to the Holy Spirit being sent to our souls. "When the Spirit of truth comes . . . he will glorify me, for he will take what is mine and declare it to you" (Jn 16: 13–14). He is sent by the Father and the Son to accomplish in us the sanctification Christ won for us here on earth. This godliness involves our resembling more and more the Son by the growth of our divine filiation.

St. Thomas Aquinas teaches that, when the Holy Spirit is sent to us, he takes up his abode in our souls "in a new way." Both sacred Scripture and tradition show the Paraclete, envoy of both the Father and the Son, as continuing and completing in some way the Son's temporal mission on earth. So Christ told us repeatedly, "It is to your advantage that I go away, for if I do not go away, the Counselor will not come to you. . . . When the Spirit of truth comes, he will guide you into all the truth" (Jn 16: 7, 13). It is he who leads to fuller understanding of what Christ taught. "He completes revelation, perfects it, and confirms it with divine witness." [1]

How is he newly present to us? Is some change wrought in the divine Person, something like a new relationship to a created person? Such cannot be. The divine Persons are unchangeable, just as is the divine essence with which each created person relates. He can be newly present to us only by means of a change in the created person.[2]

---

[1] Vatican II, *Dei Verbum*, no. 4.
[2] See Thomas Aquinas, *Summa Theologiae*, I, q. 43, a. 2, ad 2.

According to St. Thomas, this transformation consists in a special gift assimilating the created person in a particular way to the Person sent.[3] By communicating himself, the same Holy Spirit restores human nature according to the beauty of the divine model, Christ himself. That is how "we will come to know our Lord better, and at the same time, we will realize more fully the great favor that was granted us when we became Christians. We will see all the greatness and truth of the divinization, a sharing in God's own life."[4] Beside many other gifts, the Holy Spirit gives us the greatest: himself. Thereby he engoddens the soul, according to Church Fathers. "From the Holy Spirit come knowledge of future events, understanding of the mysteries, knowledge of hidden truths, distribution of gifts, heavenly citizenship, conversation with angels. From him also arise unending joy, perseverance in God, likeness to God, and the most sublime state that can be conceived, becoming Godlike."[5] In a word: godliness.[6]

## The Holy Spirit: a gift of the cross

The Holy Spirit's mission to men entails a new beginning, not unlike that of creation.[7] This new chapter or era inaugurated by the Holy Spirit does not replace that of Christ, but is linked to his departure. "It is to your advantage that I go away, for if I do not go away, the Counselor will not come to you," Jesus said (Jn 16: 7). And after the resurrection, "he sought out the apostles to breathe on them: as if preparing a new creation, the resurrected Christ 'brings' to the apostles the Holy Spirit. But he cannot bring the Spirit unless Jesus departs: as if he gave the Spirit through the wounds of the crucifixion."[8] "As a result of that

---

[3] Ibid., I, q. 43.

[4] *Christ Is Passing By*, no. 134.

[5] *Christ Is Passing By*, no. 133; St. Basil, *De Spiritu Sancto*, 9, 23 (PG 32:110).

[6] Thus the invisible missions of the Son and the Holy Spirit to the soul are not merely an appropriation or attribution, but a real participation of a spiritual creature in the eternal processions of the Son and the Holy Spirit. See Thomas Aquinas, *Summa Theologiae*, I, q. 43.

[7] See John Paul II, *Dominum et vivificantem*, no. 12.

[8] Ibid., no. 24.

sacrifice, the Holy Spirit is poured out upon mankind" (see Rom 3: 24ff; Heb 10: 5ff; Jn 7: 39).[9]

Therefore, there can be no gift of the Holy Spirit that is not a gift of Jesus, dying on the cross for us. The Holy Spirit cannot be sent without the cross and resurrection.[10] This mission initiates the era of God's children in Christ. Christ's death and resurrection make up one single reality, inseparable aspects of the same redemptive event.[11] Thus, "only when man is faithful to grace and decides to place the cross in the center of his soul, denying himself for the love of God . . . only then will he receive to overflowing the great fire, the great light, the great comfort of the Holy Spirit."[12] This new start takes place only on terrain worked by sacrifice. If one seeks to avoid the cross, sacrifice, he sacrifices this gift.

The path to identification with Christ, to divine filiation, entails therefore a growth progressing and ascending to the cross, indispensable condition for contemplation. So the saints have shown us.

## Divine filiation: work of the Holy Spirit

All Christ's life, from his conception to his glorification, each of his deeds and words, "proceeds from the fullness of the Spirit in him." This union with the Holy Spirit, "a union he is fully aware of," is the "hidden source," the "intimate font of the messianic life and actions."[13] This was the gift, an invaluable present, left to us by Christ before returning to the Father: his Spirit, the Holy Spirit.

Such is the new era of God's children. "Children of God are, in effect, as the Apostle teaches, those 'led by the Spirit of God' (Rom 8: 14). Divine filiation is born in men on the foundation

[9] *Christ Is Passing By*, no. 96.

[10] Ibid., no. 137.

[11] "The Holy Spirit will come when Christ has departed by means of the cross; he will come not only after, but because of, the redemption carried out by Christ, by will and deed of the Father." John Paul II, *Dominum et vivificantem*, no. 22.

[12] *Christ Is Passing By*, no. 137.

[13] Ibid., nos. 21–22.

of the mystery of the incarnation, that is, thanks to Christ, the eternal Son. But the birth, or rebirth, takes place when God the Father 'has sent the Spirit of his Son into our hearts' (Gal 4: 6; see also Rom 5: 5; 2 Cor 1: 22). Then, truly do we receive a Spirit of adopted children that makes us cry out 'Abba, Father!' (Rom 8: 15). Therefore, that divine filiation, which comes upon the human soul with sanctifying grace, is work of the Holy Spirit.[14] 'It is the Spirit himself bearing witness with our spirit that we are children of God, and if children, then heirs, heirs of God and fellow heirs with Christ' (Rom 8: 16–17). Sanctifying grace in man is the principle and source of the new life: divine, supernatural life."[15] Thanks to this new life, a Christian can address himself to each of the three divine Persons: to God the Father as father, to the Son as 'the first-born among many brethren' (Rom 8: 29), and to the Holy Spirit as subsistent Love of the Father and the Son, who pours out charity, love, in our hearts (see Rom 5: 5).

"God has sent the Spirit of his Son into our hearts, crying 'Abba! Father!' So through God you are no longer a slave but a son" (Gal 4: 5–6). St. Paul speaks of the presence of the three divine Persons in our supernatural life. The Father sends the Holy Spirit, here called the Spirit of the Son, who helps us understand and live the glorious reality of divine filiation. Crying out to the Father is awareness of our filiation and experiencing

[14] "The beginning of the 'new life' is wrought by means of 'the gift of divine filiation,' obtained for all by Christ with his redemption and extended to all by work of the Holy Spirit, who, in grace, remakes and 're-creates,' as it were, man in the likeness of the only-begotten Son of the Father. In this way the incarnate Word renews and consolidates the 'mutual self-giving' of God, offered to man by the redemptive deed 'participation in the divine nature,' according to the Second Letter of Peter (1:4). Likewise does St. Paul speak in the Letter to the Romans (1:4) of Jesus Christ as the one 'designated in power according to the Spirit of holiness by his resurrection from the dead.'

"The fruit of the resurrection, wrought by the plenitude of Christ's power as Son of God, is therefore offered to those who open themselves to the Spirit's action as a new gift of divine filiation. St. John, in the prologue to his Gospel (1:12), after declaring the Word became flesh, says 'to all who received him, who believed in his name, he gave power to become children of God.'

"The two apostles, John and Paul, claim that divine filiation is the gift of new life to man, by work of Christ, by the Holy Spirit." John Paul II, Address, July 26, 1989.

[15] John Paul II, *Dominum et vivificantem*, no. 52.

in our depths the tenderness of children. To say 'the Lord Jesus' is more than to utter that sweetest of names; it is to respond in our soul's intimacy to it as the yield of our mind's contemplation and as a token of our heart's love. Consequently we can declare that the Holy Spirit reveals to us our relation to the other divine Persons and leads us to love those Persons whose bond of love is the Spirit himself.

St. Paul uses the Aramaic word *Abba*, father (even daddy), the same term Christ used in his personal prayer. The Jews never dared use such familiarity in addressing God. The term reflects the tenderness and trust little children bring to their relationship with their dad. It is with such trust that our Lord wants us to turn to our heavenly Father. And Paul teaches us that the Holy Spirit no less stirs our souls to live as God's children and thus to exclaim "Abba, Father!" That is why "if we have a constant relationship with the Holy Spirit, we will become spiritual ourselves, we will realize that we are Christ's brothers and God's children, and we will not hesitate to call upon our Father at any time (see Gal 4: 6; Rom 8: 15)."[16] Thanks to the gift of piety, we shall experience that our poor soul "is moved by God's goodness. He says to us, 'You are my son.' Not a stranger, not a well-treated servant, not a friend—that would be a lot already. A son! He gives us free access to treat him as sons [would], with childlike piety and I would even say with the boldness and daring of a child whose father cannot deny him anything."[17]

We Christians are God's children because we are "led by the Spirit of God" (Rom 8: 14). Our adoptive divine filiation, source and principle of spiritual life for all the faithful, originates in the Holy Spirit. In the gift of the Spirit we receive Christ's life, the life of God's children, called to produce in us the same benefits as in Christ (see Gal 5: 22ff).

## Shaping Christ in our souls

The Holy Spirit brings forth a divine work in our souls. All his hopes are centered on each of us. At every step he gives us the

[16] *Christ Is Passing By*, no. 136.
[17] Ibid., no. 185.

graces with which to move forward: "When we struggle, God is no spectator, much as the public watches athletes. Rather, God helps us."[18] He is always in our corner; he is never neutral.

Trusting in the Holy Spirit's help leads to optimism and a victorious attitude toward our endeavors to improve. "The struggle of a child of God cannot go hand in hand with a spirit of sad-faced renunciation, somber resignation, or a lack of joy. It is, on the contrary, the struggle of someone in love who, whether working or resting, rejoicing or suffering, is always thinking of the one he loves."[19] It is a cheerful, hopeful, secure struggle.

The Holy Spirit is an artist who molds our soul into Jesus' image. If we respond and let him, he makes an authentic masterpiece of us. "For this reason, Christian tradition has summarized the attitude that we should adopt toward the Holy Spirit in just one idea: docility. That means we should be aware of the Holy Spirit's work all around us, and in our own selves we should recognize the gifts he distributes, the movements and institutions he inspires, the affections and decisions he provokes in our hearts. The Holy Spirit carries out in the world the works of God. He is, as we read in a liturgical hymn (sequence *Veni Sancte Spiritus*), the giver of grace, the light of our hearts, the soul's guest, our rest in work, our consolation in sorrow. Without his help there is nothing innocent or valuable in man, since he is the one who cleanses the soiled, heals what is sick, sets afire what is cold, straightens what is bent, and guides men toward the safe harbor of salvation and eternal joy."[20]

There is a story that one day a young boy from next door surreptitiously visited Michelangelo's studio. He could not miss seeing an enormous marble block just delivered to the sculptor. He left as silently as he had come. Months later his curiosity led him again to visit the studio. There he found, practically finished, the impressive statue of Moses. This time addressing the sculptor, he asked him how he knew that inside the marble block was the figure of Moses.

The admirable sculpture was created with the marble; but without the artist's penetrating gaze, that marble would have remained forever bereft of both grace and beauty.

[18] St. Augustine, *Sermon 128*, 9.
[19] *Friends of God*, no. 219.
[20] *Christ Is Passing By*, no. 130.

No one can outdo the Holy Spirit in *seeing* the possibilities for holiness found in each of God's children, however shapeless, however sullied, however ugly, however distorted the soul has been made by sin. First, the Holy Spirit restores God's image in man, deformed by sin, but still the root of human dignity.[21] Meanwhile, he draws forth the figure of Christ, the masterpiece of divine filiation. Moreover, unlike human sculptors who merely work externally, he intimately, from within, shapes us. "The Holy Spirit is not an artist who merely sketches on us the divine substance, as if from outside; rather it is he himself, who is God and proceeds from God, who engraves on receptive hearts the divine likeness, much like a seal on wax. By communicating himself and thus his likeness, he reestablishes human nature in keeping with the beauty of the divine model and restores man to the image of God."[22]

The stonecutter painstakingly marks on the stone the master lines the sculptor is to follow. St. Cyril teaches that the Holy Spirit's indwelling is mild and pleasing. His coming always brings with it the genuine goodness of a protector, for he comes to save, to cure, to teach, to advise, to strengthen, and to console.[23] Truly all his actions resemble the refinements mothers direct toward their children. Consequently, we must lament that the Paraclete be for some "the Great Stranger, the Great Unknown. He is merely a name that is mentioned—not someone, not one of the three Persons in the one God, with whom we can talk and with whose life we can live."[24] Truly does one rely on his beloved, whose conversation one also seeks. We are to listen, to speak, and, above all, to live with him, letting him "take possession of our lives and change our hearts, making us resemble him more and more."[25]

---

[21] This transformation is not reserved for extraordinary beings, but rather for concrete man, "in his unique and irrepeatable reality, wherein remain intact the image and likeness of God. . . . Man, just as he is 'willed' by God, 'chosen' in him from all eternity, called, destined to grace and glory . . . this very man, however mysteriously, has been made to partake of Jesus Christ." John Paul II, *Redemptor hominis*, no. 13.

[22] St. Cyril of Alexandria, *Thesaurus de sancta et consubstantiali Trinitate*, 34 (PG 75:609).

[23] St. Cyril of Jerusalem, *Catechesis 16, on the Holy Spirit*, 1.

[24] *Christ Is Passing By*, no. 134.

[25] Ibid.

A Christian ought to foster docility toward the Holy Spirit's promptings, "for if the well runs dry, we cannot supply the lack." [26] To the extent we allow it, the Paraclete forms in us good habits, virtues, little by little. Thus does the figure of Christ take shape in us, since God the Father has predestined us all to "be conformed to the image of his Son" (Rom 8: 29).

It is he who forms, conforms, us to Christ. Then, "if we are faithful to him, Jesus' own life will somehow be repeated in the life of each one of us, both in its internal development (the process of sanctification) and in our outward behavior." [27] In this internal process we participate in him by means of the love (supernatural charity) he pours out in our hearts (cf. Rom 5: 5). By charity, by making us Christlike, he leads us to acknowledge ourselves as children of God. "The Paraclete, who is Love, teaches us to saturate our life with the virtue of charity. Thus *consummati in unum*, 'made one with Christ' (Jn 17: 23), we can be among men what the Eucharist is for us, in the words of St. Augustine, 'a sign of unity, a bond of love.' " [28]

For a divinely graced soul desirous of corresponding to this love, there can be no greater union than that between itself and its Sanctifier. St. Francis de Sales claims that the slight difference between Christ and the saints is similar to that of a musical score and its interpreters. There is only one holiness, one musical composition. But each time it is played, each interpretation sounds different, personal. The Holy Spirit plays the same notes, but they sound new, in keeping with unique features and circumstances.

## The gift of piety

The Holy Spirit makes us children of God, children of the Father in the Son. Moreover, the Paraclete teaches this reality to us. By recognizing Jesus as God's Son and through our identification with him, we also recognize ourselves as such, as children, not strangers. "The action of the Paraclete within us confirms what Christ had announced—that we are children of God, that

[26] St. Teresa of Avila, *Life*, 11, 18; she adds, "The truth is we can't afford to be absent-minded, for when there is [water], we must hurry to draw it up." Though Teresa here speaks of prayer, the same advice applies to collaborating with grace.

[27] *The Forge*, no. 418.

[28] *Christ Is Passing By*, no. 87; *In Ioannis Evangelium tractatus*, 26, 13 (PL 35:1613).

we 'have not received a spirit of bondage so as to be again in fear, but . . . a spirit of adoption as sons, by virtue of which we cry, Abba! Father!' (Rom 8: 15)."[29] Through the gift of piety the Holy Spirit reaffirms in us this joyful certainty. This gift gives us a supernatural familiarity with God. We turn to him as children. And he deals with us as would a good parent—though much more so. The promise has been fulfilled: "You shall be carried upon her hip, and dandled upon her knees" (Is 66: 12).

The gift of piety entices us to deal with God with the affection of a good child and with all others as siblings belonging to the same family. Just like a toddler fondly reaches for a parent, so too must we, advised Blessed Josemaría, although "at first it will be more difficult. You must make an effort to seek out the Lord, to thank him for his fatherly and practical concern for us. Although it is not a question of sentiment, little by little God's love makes itself felt like a rustle in the soul."[30]

The Old Testament speaks of this gift in many ways: praise and petition; adoring sentiments before the infinite divine grandeur; intimately and simply confiding to our heavenly Father joys, fears, hopes. . . . We find particularly in the Psalms all the sentiments arising in the soul that trusts in God.

This childlike trust is shown especially in the prayer the Holy Spirit inspires in our heart. "Likewise the Spirit helps us in our weakness; for we do not know how to pray as we ought, but the Spirit himself intercedes for us with sighs too deep for words" (Rom 8: 26). Thanks to these stirrings we learn how to address God rightly, in a rich and varied conversation, reflecting the tones of our life. Sometimes we will complain to our Father: "Why do you hide your face?" (Ps 44: 24). Or we share with him desires for greater holiness: "I seek you, my soul thirsts for you, my flesh faints for you, as in a dry and weary land where no water is" (Ps 63: 1). Or our longing to be more united to him: "There is nothing upon earth that I desire besides you" (Ps 73: 25). Or our wanting for unwavering trust in his mercy: "How precious is your steadfast love, O God!" (Ps 36: 7).

This childlike affection leads the wise but needy child to keep on begging until he gets what he wants. At prayer our will identifies

---

[29] *Christ Is Passing By*, no. 118.

[30] Ibid., no. 8.

itself with God's, who always wants what is best for his children. This confidence makes us secure, firm, daring; it distances the anguish and worries of those who trust only in their own strength; it strengthens us to be serene in the face of obstacles.

A Christian moved by a spirit of childlike piety understands that our Father desires the best for his children, even when dressed in hardness or difficulty. He gently arranges everything. Serenity is born of trusting in divine fatherhood. Everything, even what seems irreparable, has a remedy. God has his ways.

The gift of piety also leads us to respect greatly those around us, as fellow children of God, to pity them in their needs, and to try to address them. Further, the Holy Spirit teaches us to see in others Christ himself, doing him those services and favors: "Truly I say to you, as you did it to one of the least of these my brethren, you did it to me" (Mt 25: 40). Piety for others helps us always to judge them with kindness; it inclines us quickly to pardon any offenses, however painful.

Among the benefits of the gift of piety is peace in every setting, trusting abandonment in Providence. If God takes care of everything created, how much more care will he show his children (see Mt 6: 30)? Joy is a predominate characteristic of children of God. If we dwell every day on our divine filiation, the Holy Spirit will foster ever more a childlike trust in our heavenly Father. The determination to live charitably with all will also foster the growth of this gift in our souls.

## Embracing the Holy Spirit

The Paraclete offers grace to help us be faithful. It is up to us to welcome his help and to second it with generosity and docility. Our soul's need is similar to a bodily one: our lungs must take in constant oxygen to renew our blood. Otherwise we end up asphyxiated. Whoever rejects the inspirations of the Holy Spirit ends up losing the instinct and awareness of divine filiation.

To welcome these graces means to try to carry out what the Holy Spirit inspires us to do in the intimacy of our heart: to devote ourselves completely to our duties, especially our commitments to God; to motivate ourselves decisively to acquire a particular virtue; to bear with supernatural grace and simplicity a hardship, especially one that stays around. . . . He tugs at us interiorly, often calling to mind suggestions made by a spiritual guide. The more embracing we are of these graces, the greater we ready ourselves to receive more, the easier we find it to busy ourselves in good works.

Embracing the Holy Spirit's inspirations is essential to preserving and perfecting Christ's image in our souls, as well as our supernatural fruitfulness. The seed of grace sown in our heart is capable of germinating, growing, and bringing forth fruit. However, first it must lodge in our soul, be welcomed and acted on, for "God's opportunities do not wait. They come and go. Words of life do not linger; if we do not grasp them, the devil bears them away. Satan is not lazy; rather, his eyes are always open and ready to pounce and steal any gift we ignore."[31] This entails the small sacrifice of leaving, say, one's tools in their place, going to confession on the appointed day, examining our conscience conscientiously so as to detect where we went wrong and where consequently the Holy Spirit wants us to struggle tomorrow. It also means getting up on the dot from sleep and steering a conversation away from possible criticism of an absent party.

Resistance to grace brings about in the soul what, analogously, "hail does to flowers promising abundant fruit: they barely survive, let alone produce a crop."[32] So too does Christian life wear thin and even die.

The Holy Spirit gives us infinite grace to shun deliberate venial sin and those failings, even if not sinful, that displease God. Saints display exemplary attitudes in welcoming these supernatural aids. We too receive many graces to enhance the ordinary activities of everyday life: doing all with zest, perfection, pure intention, for noble human reasons and, even better, supernatural ones. If we stay faithful to the Paraclete's inspirations, our days will be filled with loving deeds for God and neighbor, in good times or when we are consumed by tiredness and weakness: every moment is good for doing good.[33] One grace brings another in its wake—"to him who has will more be given" (Mk 4: 25)—and thus the soul waxes in goodness to the extent it responds. The farther it goes, the clearer the way becomes.

[31] Cardinal J. H. Newman, *Sermon for Sexagessima Sunday: The Calls of Grace.*

[32] R. Garrigou-Lagrange, *The Three Ages of the Interior Life,* 1:105.

[33] "Let yourself be formed by the rough or gentle strokes of grace. Strive to be an instrument rather than an obstacle. And, if you are willing, your most holy

Each day is a great God-given chance for us children to be filled with love regardless of setbacks and hardships, always counting on divine help to overcome and convert them into reasons for apostolic holiness. How much things change when we carry them out through love and for Love.

Fidelity to the Holy Spirit's inspirations is also shown in rising above the discouragement born of our failings and any impatience on seeing, say, that we are still somewhat superficial in prayer or in correcting a defect or in being aware of God's presence while at work. A farmer is patient: he does not unearth the seed or neglect the field when the desired result is long in coming. He knows well that he must work and wait, depending all the while on both rain and sun. He knows the seed is maturing, "he knows not how" (Mk 4: 27), and that harvest time will soon be upon him. "Grace, like nature, normally acts gradually. We cannot, properly speaking, get ahead of grace. But in all that does depend on us we have to prepare the way and cooperate when God grants grace to us.

"Souls have to be encouraged to aim very high; they have to be impelled toward Christ's ideal. Lead them to the highest goals, which should not be reduced or made weaker in any way. But remember that sanctity is not primarily worked out with one's own hands. Grace normally takes its time and is not inclined to act with violence.

"Encourage your holy impatience, but do not lose your patience." [34] With the wisdom of centuries, a farmer knows how to wait. We are to struggle with patient perseverance, convinced that overcoming a shortcoming or acquiring a virtue usually depends not on sporadic heroics, but on humbly continuing to struggle, counting all the while on God's mercy. We cannot, in our impatience, be unfaithful to the graces received. Such impatience is rooted, almost always, in pride.

---

Mother will help you; and you will be a channel for the waters of God, rather than a boulder that diverts their flow."

"Lord, help me to be faithful and docile toward you, *sicut lutum in manu figuli*, like clay in the potter's hands. In this way it will not be I that live, but you, my Love, who will live and work in me." *The Forge*, nos. 874, 875.

[34] *Furrow*, no. 668.

# CHAPTER 6

# God's Children in Christ: Children of Mary

## Daughter, Mother, and Spouse of God

St. Thomas teaches that Mary "is the only one, besides God the Father, who can say to the divine Son: You are my Son."[1] And St. Bernard writes that our Lady "calls Son of mine the God and Lord of the angels, when so naturally she asks, 'Son, why have you treated us so?' (Lk 2: 48). . . . Mary, always aware of being his mother, familiarly calls Son the very same sovereign majesty before whom the angels prostrate themselves. God cannot mind being called what he wished to be."[2] Truly he is Mary's son.

Christ's eternal generation (his divine procession, the Word's preexistence) is distinguished from his earthly birth. As God, he is begotten, not made, mysteriously by the Father *ab aeterno* (from always); as man, he was born, was made, of holy Mary. When came the time, God's only-begotten, the second Person of the most blessed Trinity, took to himself a human nature, that is, a reasonable soul and a body formed in Mary's womb. Human nature (body and soul) and the divine became one in the only Person of the Word. Since then, our Lady, by assenting to God's plans, became Mother of the incarnate Son of God.[3]

Since Mary is true Mother of the Son of God made man, she is directly related to the most blessed Trinity.[4] She is "daughter

---

[1] *Summa Theologiae*, III, 1, 30, a. 1.

[2] *Homilies in Praise of the Virgin Mother*, I, 7.

[3] "Just as all mothers, in whose wombs are formed our bodies but not the rational soul, are called and truly are mothers, so also Mary, thanks to the one Person of her Son, is truly God's Mother." Pius XI, *Lux veritatis*, 1931. See also Council of Ephesus, Denz 301–302.

[4] In heaven the angels and saints contemplate with amazement Mary's peerless glory, while they know well that her dignity comes from being God's Mother:

of the Father," so called by both Church Fathers and the Magisterium, both ancient and recent.[5] With the Son, the most holy Virgin has the intimate link of motherhood, "by which she acquires natural power and dominion over Jesus. . . . And Jesus contracts with Mary the duties of justice that children have for their parents." [6] With respect to the Holy Spirit, Mary is, according to the Fathers, temple and tabernacle, expressions found often in the writings of Pope John Paul II.[7] She is the "master work of the Trinity."[8] And she is hardly incidental to a Christian's life.[9]

With her motherly concern, our Lady continues to offer her Son the attentions she surrounded him with here on earth. She also does so with us, since we are members of Christ's Mystical Body. She sees Jesus in each Christian, in every person. And as co-redemptrix, on her weighs the onus of seeing us incorporated definitively to divine life. Always she will be of great help to overcome hardships and temptations, our great ally in becoming apostles.[10]

Both theology and the Marian piety of the faithful have found in Mary various relationships with the divine Persons. "How people like to be reminded of their relationship with dis-

---

*Mater Creatoris, Mater Salvatoris.* Therefore, in the Litany, the first invocation is that of *Sancta Dei Genitrix* (Holy Mother of God), and the following titles stem from her divine motherhood: Holy Virgin of Virgins, Mother of Divine Grace, Mother Most Pure, Mother Most Chaste. . . .

[5] See Vatican II, *Lumen gentium*, no. 53.

[6] E. Hugon, *Marie, pleine de grâce.*

[7] *Redemptoris Mater*, no. 9.

[8] M. M. Philipon, *Los dones del Espíritu Santo*, 382.

[9] "She's no mere person so adorned with divine gifts that we're left admiring her. This master work of the Trinity is the Redeemer's Mother and, therefore, also my mother, mother of the poor human being that I am, as is every mortal." J. Polo Carrasco, *María y la Santísima Trinidad*, 56.

[10] "Invoke the blessed Virgin. Keep asking her to show herself a mother to you—*Monstra te esse Matrem!* As well as drawing down her Son's grace, may she bring the clarity of sound doctrine to your mind, and love and purity to your heart, so that you may know the way to God and take many souls to him" (*The Forge*, no. 986). The aspiration *Monstra te esse Matrem*, taken from the liturgical hymn *Ave Maris Stella*, so often on Blessed Josemaría's lips, has helped many Christians to be united to her, especially in moments of great need.

tinguished figures in literature, in politics, in the armed forces, in the Church! Sing to Mary Immaculate, reminding her: Hail Mary, daughter of God the Father; Hail Mary, Mother of God the Son; Hail Mary, Spouse of God the Holy Spirit. . . . Greater than you, no one but God!" [11]

In the Hail Mary, Marian prayer *par excellence*, Mary is greeted as "full of grace." Since grace is what makes us children of God, this prayer underscores the grandeur of divine filiation in Mary.[12] Even the most common terminology expresses her ties with the divine Persons as daughter of God the Father, Mother of God the Son, and Spouse of God the Holy Spirit. Yet these titles are not all on the same level. That she is God's daughter does not derive from the Incarnation but from the grace of adoption, common to all those raised to the supernatural order. But the other two are directly related to the Incarnation. This had a definite date, in the fullness of time. "When the blessed Virgin said *Yes,* freely, to the plans revealed to her by the Creator, the divine Word assumed a human nature: a soul and a body, formed in the most pure womb. The divine and human natures were united in a single Person: Jesus Christ, true God and, thenceforth, true man; the only-begotten and eternal Son of the Father and, from that moment on, as man, the true son of Mary. This is why our Lady is the Mother of the incarnate Word, the second Person of the blessed Trinity who has united our human nature to himself forever, without any confusion of the two natures. The greatest praise we can give to the blessed Virgin is to address her loudly and clearly by the name that expresses her very highest dignity: Mother of God." [13]

On the other hand, Mary is Mother of God the Son and

---

[11] *The Way*, no. 496. "Only faith can shed some light on how a creature can be raised to such great heights, becoming a loving target for the delights of the Trinity. We know this is a divine secret. Yet because our Mother is involved, we feel we can understand it more—if we're entitled to speak in this way—than other truths of our faith." *Christ Is Passing By*, no. 171.

[12] "She is the *full of grace* (Lk 1:28), as greeted by St. Gabriel. Not just with many graces, but full, filled with every type of grace. Therefore the archangel adds *Dominus tecum*: the Lord is in you, in you lies all the love of God the Father, all the divine fire of the Holy Spirit, in you does the Word take on flesh." Josemaría Escrivá, *Libro de Aragón*.

[13] *Friends of God*, no. 274.

Spouse of God the Holy Spirit in different ways. She has given to the second Person of the Trinity everything a mother gives her child (and, therefore, is properly and truly Mother of the incarnate Word). Yet she did not receive from the Holy Spirit what a woman receives from her husband in conceiving a child. In no way can Christ be called son of the Holy Spirit.[14] Nevertheless, the title of Spouse of the Holy Spirit became widespread in the thirteen century and was picked up by the Church's teaching authority.

Mary is daughter of the Father in the Son by the Holy Spirit, for she was ushered by the Trinity into its intimate life in a most special way. Thus her union with subsistent divine Love (Holy Spirit) confers on her soul such full identification with the Son that, *in the Son,* she is as fully daughter of the Father as a creature can possibly be.[15]

## Going (and returning) to the Trinity through Mary

Long ago it became customary in certain places to represent our Lady with a huge cloak under whose protection were found all kinds of people: popes and kings, merchants and farmers, men and women. . . . Those not quite beneath that cloak were wounded by arrows: the representative of laziness was shown seated with an arrow through his shriveled limb; the glutton, plate in hand, was wounded in the belly.[16] When was the time when Christians did not see Mary as help and refuge for sinners? We instinctively turn to her at times of strong temptation, of severe distress or great hardship, or when perhaps we have not been faithful to God.[17]

---

[14] See St. Augustine, *De fide, spe, caritate,* 38.12 (PL 40:251-252).

[15] "Mary is united to Christ in a completely special and exceptional way, and equally is loved by this Beloved eternally, that is, in the Son consubstantial with the Father, in whom is concentrated all the glory of grace." John Paul II, *Redemptoris Mater,* no. 8.

[16] Cf. M. Trens, *María, Iconografía de la Virgen en el arte español,* 274ff.

[17] *Sancta Maria, refugium nostrum et virtus . . .* our refuge and strength. The word *refuge* comes from the Latin *fugere:* to flee from someone or something. By taking refuge one is fleeing from cold, from night's darkness, from a storm. There one seeks security, warmth, and rest. When we turn to our Lady, we find the only

In the earliest days of Christianity, the holy Fathers, in speaking of the mystery of the Word's Incarnation, often affirmed that in Mary's virginal womb a peace was reached between God and humanity. Thanks to her most special relationship with Christ, she spreads her motherhood over us, which consists of "contributing to the restoration of supernatural life in souls." [18] By her motherhood, the Virgin plays a most special role within the plan willed by God to free the world from sin. To that end, she "consecrated herself completely as 'handmaid of the Lord' to the Person and work of her Son, serving the mystery of redemption under him and with him." [19] She associated herself with Christ's expiation for all the world's sins; she suffered with him and co-redeemed in every moment of Jesus' life, particularly on Calvary, where she offered her Son to the Father, while offering herself with her Son. "Truly Mary became an 'ally of God,' by virtue of her divine motherhood, in the work of reconciliation." [20]

That is why many theologians say that Mary is somehow present at sacramental confession, where the graces of redemption are granted to us. She is alongside the path leading to this sacrament, stirring up contrition and sincerity and gently moving us to this font of grace. In Christians' efforts to get others to confession, she is the first ally. Should a child betake himself from the family home, what wouldn't his mother do to get him to return? "The Mother of God, who looked for her Son so anxiously when he was lost through no fault of her own, and experienced such great joy in finding him, will help us retrace our steps and put right whatever may be necessary when, because of our carelessness or our sins, we have been unable to recognize Christ. With her help we will know the happiness of

---

true protection from temptations, discouragement, loneliness. . . . Often one needs only to begin to pray to her for the temptation to disappear, for peace and optimism to return. We are to revel in the strength we find under our Lady's cloak. "All the sins of your life seem to be rising up against you. Don't give up hope! On the contrary, call on your holy Mother Mary, with the faith and abandonment of a child. She will bring peace to your soul." *The Way*, no. 498.

[18] Vatican II, *Lumen gentium*, no. 61.

[19] Ibid.

[20] John Paul II, *Reconciliatio et paenitentia*, no. 35.

holding him in our arms once more and telling him we will never lose him again." [21]

St. Alphonsus of Liguori says that the main role Christ entrusted to Mary is the dispensing of mercy, in which service Mary employs all her prerogatives. Blessed Josemaría Escrivá adds: "When I was young I wrote (with a conviction that coalesced around my daily visits to our Lady of the Pillar): 'To Jesus one goes and to him we return through Mary.' " [22] If our welcome to divine intimacy is possible because of the Son, it is only right that in reaching the Son we return to his Mother, to Mary. Neither can we be surprised that Christians, who go with Mary to Jesus, also follow the same path when they "*return* to him, if unfortunately they had wandered away." [23]

In this maternal task, Mary's mission is not to mitigate divine justice. Isn't God always good and merciful? Our Mother's mission, rather, is to ready our hearts to receive the graces her Son has in store for us. That is why it is always helpful to turn to her when we prepare ourselves to receive the sacrament of penance.

The Virgin always provides the shortest and most secure path to God. Mountain climbers are acquainted with what is usually the quickest and most direct route to reach a peak, a trail often arduous and accessible only to climbers in top form. That is not the case with Mary. She is a most pleasant path that does not demand special conditions. She welcomes us in any shape, even if we can barely take a step. That is when she proves to be closest to us, her children, "awakening in Christians a supernatural desire to act 'as members of the household of God' (Eph 2: 19)." [24] She bestows on us the gift of being ushered into the divine family. "Turn to our Lady—daughter, Mother, and Spouse of God and our mother as well—and ask her to obtain more graces for you from the blessed Trinity: graces of faith, hope, love, and contrition. Then when it seems that a harsh dry wind is blowing in your life, threatening to wither the flowers of your soul, they will not wither—and neither will those of your brothers." [25]

[21] *Friends of God*, no. 278.
[22] *Libro de Aragón*.
[23] Ibid.
[24] *Christ Is Passing By*, no. 139.
[25] *The Forge*, no. 227.

# Helping us to live as children of God

"Our mother," "mother of mine," "Show yourself to be a mother": such were the terms with which Blessed Josemaría often addressed the most holy Virgin. She is truly our mother, because she begot us to supernatural life.[26] Mary's motherhood "remains without lapsing . . . until all the elect have been gathered to God. Once assumed into heaven, she has kept up this saving mission, for with her manifold intercession she continues to obtain for us the gifts of eternal salvation. With love most motherly she tends to the brethren of her Son, who continue as pilgrims amid danger and anxiety till they are led to their most blessed homeland."[27]

On Calvary Jesus gave us Mary to be our mother. Nailed to the cross, he said, "'Woman, behold, your son!' Then he said to the disciple, 'Behold, your mother!'" (Jn 19: 26–27). On the edge of dying, he bequeathed us his most precious belongings, he left us "the testament of the cross."[28] This is the ultimate meaning of the solemn words we heard from the cross. They are voiced as our redemption is peaking. That is why "Christ's Mother, in the very midst of the mystery covering each and every man, is entrusted to each and every man as mother."[29] "Behold your mother" is said to each of us. John, on behalf of all, kindly took her in and cared for her with utter refinement.[30] Christ in giving us his Mother to be ours shows how deeply he loves her to the very end. By accepting the apostle John as her son, Mary shows her motherly love for all mankind.

---

[26] "Conceiving Christ, engendering him, nourishing him, presenting him to the Father in the Temple, suffering with her Son when dying on the cross, she cooperated peerlessly in the Savior's work through obedience, faith, hope, and ardent charity, so as to return supernatural life to souls. For these reasons she is our Mother in the order of grace." *Lumen gentium*, no. 61.

[27] Ibid., no. 62.

[28] John Paul II, *Redemptoris Mater*, no. 23.

[29] Ibid.

[30] John "brought Mary into his home, into his life. Spiritual writers have seen these words of the Gospel as an invitation to all Christians to bring Mary into their lives. Mary certainly wants us to invoke her, to approach her confidently, to appeal to her as our mother, asking her to 'show that you're our mother' (hymn *Ave Maris Stella*)." *Christ Is Passing By*, no. 140.

Mary's spiritual motherhood is far superior to any natural maternity. Because she gives birth to us in the supernatural order, she is our mother; by God's will, Mary is mediatrix of all graces. Supernatural life reaches us through her hands. If we have been given the power to become children of God, to participate in God's nature (see 2 Pet 1: 4), it is due to Christ's redemptive actions, which make us resemble him. But this influx reaches us through Mary. And thus, just as God the Father has but one Son through nature, and innumerable children through grace, through Mary, Christ's Mother, we have become children of God. Through her hands come all spiritual nourishment, protection against enemies, relief from pain.

Blessed Josemaría advised, "Talk to the three Persons, to God the Father, to God the Son, to God the Holy Spirit. And so as to reach the blessed Trinity, go through Mary." [31] We have received our divine filiation by means of Christ, the incarnate Word, and we behave as children because of our identification with him. Mary leads us by the hand to imitate her Son: "Our Lady, Holy Mary, will make of you *alter Christus, ipse Christus*: another Christ, Christ himself!" [32]

Devotion to Mary, expressing as it does mutual affection between mother and child, overflows with personal intimacy. "Essential to motherhood is reference to the individual. Motherhood always fixes a unique and irrepeatable relationship between two persons: the mother with the child and the child with his mother. Even when the same woman is mother of many children, her personal relationship with each of them characterizes motherhood in its very essence. In effect, each child is begotten in a unique and irrepeatable way, and this happens with respect to both parties. Each child is enveloped in the same way by her motherly love." [33] And what holds for "nature," also holds, analogously, for the "order of grace." [34] That is why

---

[31] *The Forge*, no. 543.

[32] *Christ Is Passing By*, no. 11. "Our Lady: Who could be a better teacher of God's love than this Queen, this Lady, this Mother? Isn't hers the closest bond with the Trinity: Daughter of God the Father, Mother of God the Son, Spouse of God the Holy Spirit? And yet she is our mother!" *The Forge*, no. 555.

[33] John Paul II, *Redemptoris Mater*, no. 45.

[34] Ibid., no. 23.

the affirmation that Mary becomes mother to *each disciple* enlightens the meaning of the response of the apostle John: "And from that hour the disciple took her to his own home" (Jn 19: 27). This "affirmation indicates, even though indirectly, the intimate relation of a child with his mother." [35]

Therefore, we ought to develop in ourselves the greatest possible trust in Mary. "If we truly got to know Mary our Mother, how quickly the supernatural virtues would grow in us!" [36] "There is no danger of exaggerating. We can never hope to fathom this inexpressible mystery; nor will we ever be able to give sufficient thanks to our mother for bringing us into such intimacy with the blessed Trinity." [37]

## Mediatrix of all graces

A mediator's job is to bring together, or at least to open communication between, two distant parties. Jesus Christ, God's only Son, is the only and perfect mediator between God and men (cf. 1 Tim 2: 5), because, as God and man, he offered up a sacrifice of infinite value (his own death) to reconcile men with God.[38] But this does not keep the saints, Christians in general, and, in a most particular way, our Lady from functioning as mediators.[39] The Virgin, Christ's Mother and mother of disciples

---

[35] Ibid., no. 45.

[36] *Friends of God*, no. 293. "I would recommend that, if you haven't already done so, you find out for yourself by personal experience the meaning of Mary's motherly love. It's not enough just to know she is our mother and to think and talk about her as such. She is your mother and you are her son. She loves you as if you were her only child in this world. Treat her accordingly: tell her about everything that happens to you, honor her, and love her. No one will do it for you or as well as you, if you do not do it yourself. I give you my word that, if you set out along this way, you will quickly discover all the love of Christ: and you will find yourself drawn into the ineffable life of God the Father, God the Son, and God the Holy Spirit." Ibid.

[37] Ibid., no. 276.

[38] See Thomas Aquinas, *Summa Theologiae*, III, q. 26, a. 2.

[39] "The motherly mission of Mary towards mankind in no way obscures or diminishes the unique mediation of Christ, but rather shows forth its efficacy. Every saving help by the blessed Virgin in favor of mankind is not demanded by

desirous of identifying themselves with her Son, is a singular "Mediatrix before the Mediator." [40] With respect both to Christ and to mankind hers is a motherly role. Consequently, in interceding, Mary "places herself 'in the midst,' that is, makes herself a mediator not like a stranger, but in her role as mother, aware that as such she can—rather, 'has the right to'—lay before her Son the needs of men." [41] Hers is a mediation intimately linked to her role as mother and our condition as needy children. Pope John Paul II explains in detail that "this mothering in the order of grace arises from her very divine motherhood." [42] Since she is God's Mother, our Lady finds herself, as we saw, closely related to the Trinity. And since she is mother of all mankind, she is divinely charged with caring for her pilgrim children on the way to the house of their Father.

God so wanted, teaches St. Bernard, that all good come to us through her. "It's God's will that we obtain everything through Mary," [43] declared the saint in his famous sermon likening her to an aqueduct. She "was not merely a passive instrument in God's hands, but cooperated in the salvation of men with voluntary faith and obedience." [44]

She is our primary intercessor in heaven, obtaining for us whatever we need. Moreover, she often anticipates our requests; she protects us; she inspires in the soul's depths the holiness that leads us to live charitably and with greater refinement; she stirs up contrition and penance; she heartens and strengthens us when discouragement threatens. She is there to defend us the moment we turn to her. . . . She is our great ally in our apostolic efforts; specifically, she turns our inadequate words into an eloquence that spurs our friends' hearts. Many saints have discovered that with Mary we attain supernatural objects "sooner, more, and better" than we had any reason to believe.

---

any law, but rather is born of her goodwill and the superabundance of Christ's merits." Vatican II, *Lumen gentium*, no. 60.

[40] St. Bernard, *Sermon 2, Sunday within the Octave of the Assumption.*

[41] John Paul II, *Redemptoris Mater*, no. 21.

[42] Ibid., no. 6.

[43] *Sermon on the Aqueduct.*

[44] Vatican II, *Lumen gentium*, no. 56.

# Our father and lord

The evangelists call Joseph "father" on several occasions (Lk 2: 27, 33, 41, 48). Without a doubt this is the name Jesus habitually used in the intimacy of his Nazareth home whenever he addressed the holy patriarch. By all who knew him, Jesus was considered "Joseph's son" (see Lk 3: 23). Indeed Joseph discharged the role of father in the Holy Family. We see this when he named Jesus, when they fled to Egypt, when choosing where to live on their return. . . . And Jesus obeyed Joseph as a father: "He went down with them and came to Nazareth, and was obedient to them" (Lk 2: 51).

Jesus was conceived miraculously by the Holy Spirit and was virginally born to Mary and Joseph by divine decree. God wanted Jesus to grow up in a family, submissive to a father and mother, who also cared for him. Just as he chose Mary to be mother, he also chose Joseph to be father, each with a distinct role.[45]

St. Joseph had true fatherly sentiments for Jesus. Grace enabled that willing and ready heart of his to love ardently God's Son, more than would have been the case of a natural son. Joseph cared for Jesus, loving him as a son, adoring him as his God. And the spectacle, ever before his eyes, of a God raining his

[45] Blessed Josemaría was not shy in affirming the wonderful qualities God had given to Joseph. He would ask whether St. Joseph had been perfect, and he would answer: "Yes, he'd have to be. . . . I find no reason not to use in his behalf the argument employed to justify Mary's God-given prerogatives: *potuit, decuit, ergo fecit*. . . . God could choose his Mother, adorning her with beauty, wisdom, grace . . . it was fitting that he do so; therefore, he did so. Wouldn't you have done so? And I? Of course! Could it possibly be that God's heart is smaller than ours? No!

"God had to choose a man, a wonderful man. . . . He does so, from all eternity. . . . So did he choose us: *elegit nos ante mundi constitutionem, ut essemus sancti in conspectu eius*. Well, if he so chose us, could he do less for him who would father him here on earth, who would protect him, who would feed him with his work, who would take him here and there to avoid Herod's persecution? Doesn't that seem right to you? So, then, he'd also fill him with virtues, for such was fitting. I am convinced that Holy Mary is the most beautiful of creatures—greater than she, none but God—but right after her comes St. Joseph. They can't be separated." From a get-together in Brazil with Blessed Josemaría in 1974 and cited in L. M. Herrán, *La devoción a San José en la vida y enseñanzas de Mons. Escrivá de Balaguer.*

infinite love on the world spurred him to love Jesus more and more.

St. Joseph's patronage over the Church and each Christian merely prolongs the cares he multiplied for Jesus Christ and Mary, Mother of Jesus, and of his Mystical Body. That is why he was named "universal patron of the Church."[46] St. Joseph's mission is lengthened through the centuries. His fatherhood reaches each of us.[47] He who acted as Jesus' father plays an equally fatherly role for those who wish to identify themselves with Christ, for children of God.[48] Thus, said Blessed Josemaría Escrivá, "I try to reach heaven's Trinity by that other *earthly* trinity: Jesus, Mary, and Joseph."[49] With this childlike familiarity, Mary and Joseph lead us to Jesus and teach us to identify ourselves with him.

[46] Pius IX, *Quemadmodum Deus; Inclytum Patriarcam.*

[47] Welcomed into Joseph's family (as a child of God), it pleased Blessed Josemaría to call him "father and lord," recognizing him as protector and patron. "For centuries many different features of his life have caught the attention of believers. He was a man ever faithful to the mission God gave him. That's why, for many years now, I have liked to address him fondly as 'our father and lord.'

"St. Joseph really is father and lord. He protects those who revere him and accompanies them on their journey through this life—just as he protected and accompanied Jesus when he was growing up. As you get to know him, you discover that the holy patriarch is also master of the interior life—for he teaches us to know Jesus and share our life with him, and to realize that we are part of God's family." *Christ Is Passing By*, no. 39.

[48] While meditating on the Gospel on the way St. Joseph acted, Blessed Josemaría claimed that the holy patriarch was the sure path, in the company of Mary, to reach identification with Christ. "I like to go back in my imagination to the years Jesus spent close to his Mother, years spanning almost the whole of his life on earth. I like to picture him as a little child, cared for by Mary who kisses him and plays with him. I like to see him growing up before the loving eyes of his Mother and of Joseph, his father on earth. What tenderness and care Mary and the holy patriarch must have shown toward Jesus, as they looked after him during his childhood, all the while, silently, learning so much from him. Their souls would become more and more like the soul of that Son, who was both man and God. That's why his Mother, and after her, St. Joseph, understand better than anyone the feelings of the Heart of Christ; and the two of them are, therefore, the best way, I would say the only way, to reach the Savior." *Friends of God*, no. 281.

[49] Josemaría Escrivá, Homily, March 28, 1975; in S. Bernal, *Apuntes sobre la vida del Fundador del Opus Dei*, 316–319.

# CHAPTER 7

# Children of God:
# Offspring of the Church

## Christ in the Church

The mission of the Son of God did not end with his return to heaven. Jesus is not just an historical figure who lived, died, and was resurrected to be exalted at the right hand of God the Father. Rather, he continues to live today among us in a real, though mysterious, way.

*Yesterday* he lived with men, in a concrete historical past. *Today* he lives in heaven, at the right hand of the Father, and he also lives *today* at our side, continually feeding us life by means of the sacraments, while accompanying us in a real way through the ups and downs of our quest. Christ's most holy humanity was not assumed just for a few decades. The Incarnation was decreed from all eternity, and God's Son, born of the Virgin Mary in time and history, in the days of Augustus Caesar, remains a man forever, with a glorious body, resplendent with the wounds of his Passion.

Raised and glorious, Christ lives in heaven and, in a mysterious but real way, also in his Church. The Church is an extension of the person of Christ in both time and space. The Church makes Christ present to and for us; there we find him. The Church's grandeur lies in this intimate link to Christ; that is why the reality is an indescribable mystery. No human terms can express the unique richness that originates in the very Person of Jesus and is aimed at perpetuating his saving presence among us. Even more, the sole mission of the Church is to make Christ present, he who returned to heaven but promised to be "with you always, to the close of the age" (Mt 28: 20), and to lead us to him.

The Church offers us occasions to find God. The Church has mothered all the saints throughout the centuries. First were the martyrs, who gave their lives in witness to the faith they professed. Then the history of humanity has been stirred by the example of so many women and men who lovingly gave their lives to help their brethren in all their needs and difficulties. Name an example of human wretchedness that has not awoken in the Church the call of men and women to remedy it, often to the point of heroism. Many are the parents, even today, who spend their lives silently but heroically guiding their families along in fulfillment of a call from God. There are also men and women who, amid the world, live committed to God, as celibates or virgins while still ordinary citizens. They give special joy and glory to God, hallowing their varied occupations and apostolically spurring their colleagues.

It can be said of the Church, in a certain sense, what is said of Christ: he is from above, not from below; his origin is divine. The Church is no earthly grouping, no cultural font, no political force, no scientific school; she is created by the heavenly Father through Jesus Christ.

No one can be God's good child without being so of the Church. How can one love Christ mightily without so loving his Mystical Body? Interior growth, holiness, necessarily brings in its wake greater unity and love for the Church. This love of a child leads a Christian to see the Church with eyes of faith: thus does she appear spotless, holy, without wear or wrinkles. A Christian will not tolerate that the Church be viewed as just another mortal human society, oblivious to the profound mystery pulsating within.

Holy is the Church, because her children, God's children, are called to holiness. The Church's sanctity, moreover, is something permanent, independent of the number of Christians who live their faith to the fullest. She is holy through the continual presence of the Holy Spirit within, and not by the behavior of men. That is why, even in the gravest moments, "even if gross infidelities were to outnumber the valiant faithful, there would still remain that mystical reality—clear, undeniable, even if invisible to human senses—which is Christ's Body, our very Lord, the action of the Holy Spirit, the loving presence of the Father." [1]

---

[1] Josemaría Escrivá, *Amar a la Iglesia*, 47.

Born of this love for the Church, with its firm theological grounding, is the ease with which its good children pray and sacrifice themselves daily for its sake. What might a good child do? Dedicate, for example, a decade of the rosary; offer up hours of work or study or physical pain or tribulations; earnest petition to her at Mass. . . .

## The Church our Mother

What authorizes us to call the Church Mother? "The Church hallows us, having been welcomed to her lap by baptism. Just having been born to natural life, we soon grasp onto sanctifying grace. 'The faith of one member, nay, the faith of the entire Church, benefits the baby by deeds of the Holy Spirit, who unifies the Church and spreads the gifts of one to another.'[2] How wonderful is the spiritual motherhood conferred on the Church by the Paraclete. 'Spiritual regeneration, brought about by baptism, somehow resembles corporal birth. Children still in their mothers' womb cannot feed themselves, but rather live off nourishment provided by their mothers. Isn't that similar to infants who before the age of reason are harbored in the Church's lap? Thanks to the action of the Church (and not through their own endeavors), salvation is fed to them, so to speak.'"[3]

Where do we find the root of the Church's motherhood? We find it in her holiness, in her ability to give life and to restore it, should it be lost. Our divine filiation stems from and in her, born as it is with baptism. People came from afar to find in Jesus someone who could authoritatively speak to them of the Father; they find in him their teacher. And we find ourselves ever more linked to him by accepting the Church's teaching: "He who hears you hears me, and he who rejects you rejects me" (Lk 10: 16).

Moreover, Jesus is our Redeemer. He is a priest, possessed of the only priesthood, who offered himself to undo our sins. "So also Christ did not exalt himself to be made a high priest, but was appointed by him who said to him, 'You are my Son'" (Heb

---

[2] Thomas Aquinas, *Summa Theologiae*, III, q. 68, a. 9, ad 2.
[3] *Amar a la Iglesia*, 32–33; *Summa Theologiae*, III, q. 68, a. 9, ad 1.

5: 5). To Jesus, priest and victim, who honors God the Father while drawing us to him, we unite ourselves to the degree we take part in the Church's life, especially of its sacraments, those divine channels whereby grace reaches souls. Whenever we receive them, we touch Christ himself, source of every grace. By means of the sacraments, the infinite merits Christ won for us strengthen persons of every age and, therefore, constitute firm hope of eternal life. In the holy Eucharist, which Christ instructed that the Church celebrate, we renew his oblation and immolation. "This is my body which is given for you. Do this in remembrance of me" (Lk 22: 19). The Eucharist nourishes us with life, whose very source is Jesus himself: "If any one eats of this bread, he will live forever; and the bread which I shall give for the life of the world is my flesh" (Jn 6: 51).

Baptism is the beginning of our lives as children of God: "Go therefore and make disciples of all nations, baptizing them in the name of the Father and of the Son and of the Holy Spirit" (Mt 28: 19). "He who believes and is baptized will be saved" (Mk 16: 16). And if our wrongs have distanced us from God, the Church is the means by which we again become the Lord's living members: "If you forgive the sins of any, they are forgiven; if you retain the sins of any, they are retained" (Jn 20: 23). Jesus established that the very deepest links with him be developed through the visible signs of the Church's sacramental life. In the Church we are born and reborn in Christ.

To reach heaven, to consummate our divine filiation, to partake wholly of God's intimate life, we must be born to God's life in baptism; and that birth introduces us to the Church. Our birth as God's children is *ex Deo* (of God), but it is also *ex Ecclesia* (of the Church). We are the Church's children to the extent we are God's children; and vice versa. Moreover, Christ started *the* Church, his Church, his only spouse. For the Church to be mother, she must have unity.

Only by being united to Christ, to the vine, do we live and give fruit. Our life is *his* life, God's life: godliness. "Now we'll understand better how the Church's oneness leads to holiness and how one of the capital aspects of her sanctity is that unity centered on the mystery of the triune God: 'one body and one spirit, so were you called to the very hope of your calling; one is the Lord, one the faith, one baptism, one is God and Father of all, he who is above all and governs all things while dwelling in all of us.' " [4]

Holiness means union with Christ. "The more intimate we are with our Lord, the greater our holiness. The Church was willed and founded by Christ, who thus fulfills the Father's will; the Son's spouse is vivified by the Holy Spirit. The Church is work of the most holy Trinity; she is holy and mother, our holy Mother the Church." [5]

She is "holy, because she was formed pure and will continue spotless through all eternity. . . . Our mother is holy, with Christ's holiness, to which head the body, all of us, is united and to its spirit, which is the Holy Spirit, dwelling also in the heart of each of us, so long as we cling to God's grace." [6]

Thus does the Church's motherhood manifest God's fatherhood over his adopted children. "How consoling it is to read in the ancient Fathers those complimentary outbursts of burning love for Christ's Church! 'Let us love the Lord our God; let us love his Church,' writes St. Augustine. 'Him we love as Father; her as Mother. . . .' [7] St. Cyprian was also moved to declare succinctly: 'No one can have God as Father who does not hold the Church as Mother.' " [8]

## Communion of Saints

Since we are children of the same mother by partaking of the same life, our prayer, any aridity experienced in habitual practices of piety, our weariness, our work and studies, the small discomforts every day brings—all this, and much more, can sustain so many brothers of ours in the most distant places and still others, perhaps distant from God, who can find the path, thanks to our supernatural help. [9] This train of thought will often spur us to begin anew or to practice a virtue with greater refinement, to pray

[4] *Amar a la Iglesia*, 19; St. Cyprian, *De catholicae Ecclesiae unitate*, 6 (PL 4:503).

[5] *Amar a la Iglesia*, 19.

[6] Ibid., 24.

[7] St. Augustine, *Enarrationes in Psalmos*, 88, 2, 14 (PL 37:1140).

[8] *Amar a la Iglesia*, 54; *De catholicae Ecclesiae unitate*, 6 (PL 4:502).

[9] "You will find it easier to do your duty if you think of how many brothers are helping you, and of the help you fail to give them when you are not faithful." *The Way*, no. 549.

more earnestly. . . . The desire not to be a drag on others is reason enough for a Christian to strengthen one's struggle to be a saint.

Each of the faithful, with his good deeds, with his effort to be closer to God, enriches his brothers and sisters in the Church, while he also draws from the common treasure. "This is the Communion of the Saints that we profess in the Creed; the goodness of all becomes the good of each, while the goodness of each becomes good for all." [10] In a real but mysterious fashion, with our personal holiness we are contributing to the supernatural life of our brethren. Every day we both give and receive abundantly. Our life is a continual exchange of both the human and supernatural.

Each of the faithful should be joyfully aware of belonging to the Church and enjoy a universal outlook, however tiny may be the village or hospital room enveloping him. God so wants us to view things, in this way. But if a Christian were to suffer from a narrow outlook, it would be very hard for him not to belittle his calling. He would tend to be centered on himself, rather than on God and others. However alone or apart, a Christian's heart is sending good, clean blood, supernatural life, to all his brothers and sisters in Christ, especially to those most in need.

Also bolstering our hope is the help reaching us from "the witnesses who have preceded us into the kingdom (cf. Heb 12: 1), especially those whom the Church recognizes as saints"; they "share in the living tradition of prayer by the example of their lives, the transmission of their writings, and their prayer today. They contemplate God, praise him, and constantly care for those whom they have left on earth. When they entered into the joy of their Master, they were 'put in charge of many things' (Mt 25: 21). Their intercession is their most exalted service to God's plan. We can and should ask them to intercede for us and for the whole world." [11]

## Pope: father and teacher to God's children

Our filiation to the Church manifests itself through our filiation to Christ's vicar. "No one in the Church enjoys by himself, in-

---

[10] John Paul II, *Christifideles laici*, no. 28.
[11] *Catechism of the Catholic Church*, no. 2683.

sofar as man, absolute power; in the Church the only head is Christ, and Christ established a vicar of his, the Roman Pontiff, for his pilgrim Church on earth."[12]

God's children, the Church's children, are children of the Roman Pontiff. Indeed our love for God passes through our love for the Church. And our love for the Church is shown by our love for the Pope. "This should be a beautiful passion in us, because in the Pope we see Christ. If we acquaint ourselves with God in prayer, we'll go forward with a cleansed gaze to help us distinguish, even amid events opaque to us or causing grief or pain, the hand of the Holy Spirit."[13]

"St. Ambrose gave us a formula that rings of joy: 'Where Peter, there the Church; and where the Church, there reigns, not death, but life everlasting.'[14] Where we find Peter and the Church, there we find Christ, and he is salvation, the only path."[15]

The unity between Christ and the Church his spouse, and subsequently her holiness and that of her offspring, is something we foster by "venerating this spotless mother of ours and by loving the Roman Pontiff."[16] On earth he serves in lieu of Christ: his vicar. For Christians he is Jesus' tangible presence, whom St. Catherine of Siena called "the sweet Christ on earth." That is why it is hard not to love him. But we are to learn to love him effectively, with deeds: prayer and sacrifice most particularly. This love should manifest itself especially at certain times: during one of his apostolic trips, when illness overcomes him, when he is challenged by Church enemies, whenever we find ourselves near him. . . .


## Love for and filiation with the hierarchy

Love for the Church will also authenticate itself in appreciation and prayer for bishops and priests, on whom God is counting so much, since in large measure on them rests the spiritual health

---

[12] *Amar a la Iglesia,* 31.
[13] Ibid., 32.
[14] *In XII Ps. Enarratio,* 40, 30.
[15] *Amar a la Iglesia,* 29.
[16] Ibid., 18.

of the faithful. Bishops, in union with the Pope, have been commissioned by Christ himself to guide and shepherd the Church.[17] So much depends on their union with the Good Shepherd.

A good Christian cannot shrug his shoulders at criticism of the Pope, bishops, priests, religious. . . . If shortcomings and mistakes on the part of those who should be more exemplary are visible at times, a good Christian will teach others to understand and overlook them, while both pointing out attributes and praying more for them. And, whenever possible and wise, he may support them by correcting them as positively as lovingly. Never will he attribute to the Church the erring and weakness of some of her members.[18]

[17] See Vatican II, *Christus Dominus*, no. 16.

[18] "May you never fall into the error of identifying Christ's Mystical Body with a particular personal or public attitude of any of its members. And may you never let other people with less information fall into that error. Now you realize the importance of your integrity, of your loyalty." *Furrow*, no. 356.

# CHAPTER 8

# Spiritual Paternity and Fraternity

## All fatherhood from God

In the fullest sense of the word, there is but one Father, our heavenly Father (see Mt 23: 8–12), from whom stems all fatherhood in heaven and on earth (see Eph 3: 15). *"Tam Pater nemo"* (No one is so Father as God), wrote Tertullian. He is the fullest of paternity; of his have our parents partaken, as have those who in a way have begotten us to the life of faith. St. Paul lived this paternity in depth, and so he could write to the first Christians of Corinth "as my beloved children. For though you have countless guides in Christ, you do not have many fathers. For I became your father in Christ Jesus through the Gospel. I urge you, then, be imitators of me" (1 Cor 4: 14–16). The Apostle's abounding love can only be explained by the spiritual fatherhood—stronger than that of blood—he feels for the faithful. Those first Christians saw reflected in St. Paul God's loving solicitude for them.

On another occasion he wrote to the pioneering faithful of Galatia, as would a father or a mother, after he was informed of their hardships but was unable to tend to them because of the long distance. "My little children, with whom I am again in travail until Christ be formed in you!" (Gal 4: 19). Weighing on the Apostle was the worry of a father who sees his children in distress. We are therefore warranted in using the term "father" as much in the spiritual realm as in the physical. When we honor our parents, who gave us life, and those who gave us faith, we glorify God, for in them is reflected divine fatherhood. One of the ways we are to behave as God's good children is by honoring those whom God himself set up as our parents here on earth.

In the Church those who introduced us to the faith through preaching and baptism are recognized as spiritual parents.[1] This spiritual fatherhood and motherhood flourishes whenever we help others to find Christ in their lives. The more Christians are dedicated to it, the fuller this fatherhood becomes. This gift is a big part of the reward God bestows on those who follow him closely. "He is generous. He returns a hundredfold; and he does so even in children. Many deprive themselves of children for the sake of his glory, and they have thousands of children of their spirit—children, as we are children of our Father in heaven."[2]

## A father's heart

Blessed Josemaría, in imitation of Christ, could make his own our Lord's words, "I am the good shepherd. The good shepherd lays down his life for the sheep" (Jn 10: 11). Besides the grace to found Opus Dei, God also granted him the gift of spiritual fatherhood over the many thousands whom he encouraged in their faith and dedication to God by means of his example and teaching. He himself said he took on this paternity "with the full conviction of being on earth only to carry it out. Thus," he wrote to his sons and daughters of Opus Dei, "I love you with a heart both fatherly and motherly."[3] And he added he had given birth to them "like mothers, with pain, as mothers do."[4] He echoes St. Paul: "Who is weak, and I am not weak? Who is made to fall, and I am not indignant?" (2 Cor 11: 29). The Apostle remains a timeless model for those charged with caring for souls, for all apostolic Christians, since they "ought to care as fathers in Christ for the faithful begotten by baptism and doctrine."[5]

---

[1] *Roman Catechism*, III, 5, 8.

[2] *The Way*, no. 779.

[3] Letter, May 6, 1945, cited by A. Vázquez de Prada, *El Fundador del Opus Dei*, 340.

[4] Ibid., 341.

[5] Vatican II, *Lumen gentium*, no. 28. Expressly referring to the priesthood, John Paul II says that a priest "has to be able to love people with a new, pure, and big heart, with authentic renunciation, with entire dedication, as habitual as it is faithful, and with a kind of divine zeal (see 2 Cor 11:2), with a tenderness that at

Love for those we have drawn to God is not mere friendship; it is the same love with which they are loved by the incarnate Word, one that "generates in us the same desire Christ had: for their sanctification and salvation."[6] We are moved to love them more, eager to provide for them whatever may lead toward their holiness: a good example, an opportune suggestion, joy and optimism, advice that soothes their anxiety. . . . And they should always be able to count on the biggest help we can give them: our prayer.

Caring for those whom, for whatever circumstances, God has entrusted to us as their spiritual parent will help us understand the untiring solicitude God our Father has for each of us. Moreover, often our responsibility for them is reason enough to reinforce our fidelity to God and to help us move ahead on our path to holiness, like a good shepherd.

By dwelling on God's fatherhood, we will learn how to have a fatherly and motherly heart, especially for those having a hard time who seek us out. What joy to be able to say, "This my son was dead, and is alive again" (Lk 15: 24)! For whoever is hobbling, no trouble or understanding can be spared, for, like the father of the prodigal son, we must seek out those who have lost sight of God's love and thus are distancing themselves from the "Father's home." And if we behave in this way toward those who have not been all that generous, how much more should we be willing to do for those who had been faithful to God throughout both good days and bad?

Dwelling often on this spiritual fatherhood and motherhood will lead us to beg of God a merciful, welcoming heart, one prone to pity others in their needs, one that eases the return to God, to a dedicated life, for those who have strayed.[7] "Mercy," explains Pope John Paul II, "is an indispensable element to ground mutual human relations in a spirit of deepest respect for what is human, leading to mutual brotherhood. . . . Merciful

---

times resembles motherly kindness, taking on birth's 'travail' so long as Christ is not 'formed' in them (Gal 4:19)." *Pastores dabo vobis*, no. 22.

[6] B. Perquin, *Abba, Father*, 328.

[7] "Mercy means keeping one's heart totally alive, throbbing in a way that is both human and divine, with a love that is strong, self-sacrificing, and generous." *Friends of God*, no. 232.

love also implies the cordial tenderness and sensitivity we see so eloquently portrayed in the parables of the prodigal son, of the lost sheep, or of the misplaced coin." [8]

Never can we afford to be too "formal" when trying to guide others spiritually (family members, friends, colleagues . . .), especially when their sad state evokes that of the prodigal son. St. Francis de Sales advises confessors: "Even though the wasteful son returned disheveled, dirty, and smelly from having worked with pigs, the father thinks nothing of embracing and kissing him lovingly, while sobbing on his shoulder. He was the boy's father after all. How could he be anything other than tender in welcoming his son back?" [9] Such qualities also should distinguish every Christian in his apostolic care for others. [10]

## All purchased at the same price

All of us were redeemed at a high price, the price of the cross. Since then, "once the redemption had been accomplished, 'there is neither male nor female'—there is no discrimination of any type—for you are all one in Christ Jesus (Gal 3: 28)." [11] Christ came to save all. "Not just the rich, not just the poor, but everyone: all the brethren. We are all brothers in Jesus, children of God, brothers of Christ. His Mother is our mother. There is only one race in the world: the race of children of God. We should all speak the same language, taught us by our Father in heaven." [12]

[8] *Dives in misericordia*, no. 12.

[9] *Advice for Confessors*, nos. 2, 3.

[10] St. Thomas, who often insists that divine fatherhood and omnipotence especially shine forth from mercy (see *Summa Theologiae*, I, q. 21, a. 4; II-II, q. 30, a. 4), simply but graphically teaches how God's mercy abounds infinitely: "To say that someone is merciful is to say that his heart is full of misery (*misereor cor*), that is, in the face of others' wretchedness, he feels the same sadness as if the misfortune were his. That is the proper effect of mercy. Now, while we cannot say that God is saddened by our wretchedness, nothing could be more divine than to remedy our wretchedness" (I, q. 21, a. 3). A Christian has a merciful heart if with those in need he tries to echo what Christ would do in that situation.

[11] *Christ Is Passing By*, no. 38.

[12] Ibid., no. 13.

Divine filiation means we have the same Father and thus are all brothers and sisters. A shared filiation is the foundation for the fraternity of children of God among themselves and with Christ, the first-born of all the brethren.

Our brotherhood is as real as our filiation. The parallel is so close that our behaving as brothers with our siblings, as children of God with other children of God, "is not a cliché or an empty dream";[13] it has repercussions throughout our everyday life.

Born through the grace of the Father, our brotherhood possesses such a firm foundation that the link stemming from it is stronger than that born of our sharing the same human nature. This new union in Christ far exceeds the universal human fraternity. While mystical, it is nonetheless real and profound. More than being many brethren, we are in fact only one: *ipse Christus*. Unity is thus a specific feature of our fraternity, all made possible by the love poured into our hearts by the Holy Spirit.

This brotherhood is derived from a single source, Christ, and is inseparable from the love that we ought to have for our brothers and sisters. "What respect, veneration, and affection we should feel for every single soul when we realize that God loves it as his very own."[14] Charity "is, as it were, a letter of introduction proving that one is truly a son of God."[15]

## Christ's new commandment

All of Christian life should bear the seal of divine filiation: to *believe* is to see all things in the light of the Son of God; to *hope* is to tend toward possessing God, convinced that our Father God will not forget us and provide what we need; to *love* is to surround God with childlike and trusting sentiments, to desire his glory, to fulfill his will, loving all our brothers in Christ, as children of the same Father. Love, as filial as fraternal, should be the distinguishing characteristic of the family of the children of God.

After reminding us of how tenderly God the Father has loved

---

[13] *Friends of God*, no. 233.

[14] *The Forge*, no. 34.

[15] *Friends of God*, no. 44.

us in making us his children (1 Jn 3: 1), St. John summarizes how we should conduct ourselves: "This is the message which you have heard from the beginning, that we should love one another. . . . We know that we have passed out of death into life, because we love the brethren" (1 Jn 3: 11–14). The beloved apostle merely echoes the Master's teaching that charity is the certain sign of his true followers: "By this will all men know that you are my disciples, if you have love for one another" (Jn 13: 35).[16] "Love one another, even as I have loved you" (Jn 13: 34): that is, even giving up your life for your brethren, as I give up mine for you. Since then we have known that "charity is the way to follow God most closely"[17] and to find him most promptly. A soul understands God better when it lives charitably, because God is Love. We improve ourselves more and more as we grow in this theological virtue.

How we deal with those at our side is the telltale sign that we are Christ's disciples. Our union with God is calibrated by how understanding we are of others, how we deal with and serve them. We should be known as Jesus' disciples by the kind, understanding, and accommodating way we act with our peers. We will behave as true followers of Christ if we always try to be charitable in thought, word, and deed; if we right everyone we have wronged; if we generate tokens of charity with those alongside us: cordiality, esteem, encouraging words, a habitual smile and good humor, favors, true concern for their troubles, helping them in ways they will never know. . . . "This charity is to be sought not only in important moments, but above all in ordinary life."[18] Charity, love for God and souls, is the secret of spiritually helping others and of holiness.[19]

---

[16] "Let us now consider the Master and his disciples gathered together in the intimacy of the Upper Room. The time of his passion is drawing close, and he is surrounded by those he loves. The fire in Christ's heart bursts into flame in a way no words can express and he confides in them, 'I give you a new commandment: that you love one another, just as I have loved you, you also must love one another. By this shall all men know that you are my disciples, if you have love for one another' (Jn 13:34–35)." *Friends of God*, no. 222.

[17] Thomas Aquinas, *Commentary on the Epistle to the Ephesians*, 5.1.

[18] Vatican II, *Gaudium et spes*, no. 38.

[19] "Charity is the soul of the holiness to which all are called: 'it directs all the means of sanctification, it informs them and leads them to the end.' " Vatican II,

# Children of God with children of God

Like all virtues, charity is something to be lived. "Love means deeds and not sweet words"; and deeds are what Blessed Josemaría called for.[20] God shows himself to be lovingly demanding when he asks for facts, deeds, because "not every one who says to me, 'Lord, Lord,' shall enter the kingdom of heaven" (Mt 7: 21).

The manifestations of this fraternity (unity and love in Christ) in ordinary life are countless. But the root from which they stem is none other than divine filiation. "Be mindful of what others are—and first of all those at our side: children of God, with all the dignity that marvelous title entails."[21] That is how we are to look upon those near us.

We are to imitate Christ, to identify ourselves with him and in his unlimited love, with the infallible certainty that it is he who loves through us his brethren, our brothers. That is why we are to strive to view others as our Lord does, "with the very eyes of Christ."[22] With how much understanding did Jesus look upon those crowding in on him? His hopes rested on each of them. His goodness would evoke how a parent views his child, whom he is always ready to help.

A faith-filled gaze will lead us to see in others what is best in them. Our apostolic instinct should be optimistic, overflowing with supernatural sense; it should hearten and invite a new start.

Let us start by imitating Christ in the way he dealt with others, being "very human and very divine, struggling each day to

---

Lumen gentium, 42. "I understood that if the Church is a body, composed of different members, the most necessary and noble member could not be missing. I understood that the Church has a heart and that heart is *ablaze with love*. I understood that love alone can spur members of the Church, such that if love were to die out, the apostles would not spread the Good News, that martyrs would not be willing to spill their blood. . . . I understood that *love encompasses all callings, that love was everything, that it embraces all times and places. . . . In a word, love is eternal!*" St. Teresa of Avila, autobiographical manuscript, cited by the *Catechism of the Catholic Church*, no. 826.

[20] *The Forge*, no. 498.

[21] *Christ Is Passing By*, no. 36.

[22] John Paul II, *Redemptor hominis*, no. 18.

imitate him who is *perfectus Deus, perfectus homo*."[23] Christ "comes to save, not to destroy nature. It is from him that we learn that it is unchristian to treat our fellow men badly, for they are God's creatures, made to his image and likeness" (see Gen 1: 26).[24]

Every good God grants us ought to be a good for others: our mind, winning ways, our heart, every virtue. "No virtue worthy of its name can foster selfishness. Every virtue necessarily works to the good both of our own soul and to the good of those around us. We are all children of God, and we cannot think that life consists in building up a brilliant *curriculum vitae* or an outstanding career. Ties of solidarity should bind us all and, besides, in the order of grace we are united by the supernatural bond of the Communion of Saints."[25] If a Christian does not love with deeds, he has failed as a Christian, which is to fail in everything. "We have to behave as God's children toward all God's sons and daughters. Our love has to be a dedicated love, practiced every day and made up of a thousand little details of understanding, hidden sacrifice, and unnoticed self-giving."[26]

Conducting ourselves as children of God with children of God—that summarizes the fraternal charity rooted in divine filiation. This supernatural foundation calls for the requirements of love and respect for others called for by Christ's image in them. When all is said and done, ours is love and respect for Christ himself.[27]

## Brothers to all men

To get along with everybody, to love everybody, to understand everybody . . . Isn't that too much? Every last one of them is

---

[23] *Friends of God*, no. 75.

[24] Ibid., no. 73.

[25] Ibid., no. 76.

[26] *Christ Is Passing By*, no. 36.

[27] "Our love is not to be confused with sentimentality or mere good fellowship, nor with that somewhat questionable zeal to help others in order to convince ourselves of our superiority. Rather, it means living in peace with our neighbor, venerating the image of God found in each and every man and doing all we can to get them in their turn to contemplate that image, so that they may learn how to turn to Christ." *The Forge*, no. 230.

God's child, but not all are truly God's children by grace, partakers of the divine nature and intimacy. Children of God are those fully in communion with their Father, but our fraternity is extended to all persons. They too are God's children, insofar as they were created in his image and likeness and have been redeemed by Christ; likewise they are called to the intimacy of the Father's house. If they are apart from God, all the more reason to outdo ourselves in living charitably with them.[28] The first duty of charity with them is to help them live in keeping with their dignity as God's children. This is the first service, the first and best way of identifying ourselves with Christ in his charity: to co-redeem with him.

First let us spiritually help those to be children of God who till now have been only servants (cf. Jn 15: 15). God asks, demands, this simple favor of his children. "If we are to serve others, for Christ's sake, we need to be very human. If our life is less than human, God will not build anything on it, for he usually does not build on disorder, selfishness, or emptiness. We have to understand everyone; we must live peaceably with everyone; we must forgive everyone. We shall not call injustice justice; neither shall we say that an offense against God is not an offense against God, or that evil is good. When confronted by evil, we shall not reply with another evil, but rather with sound doctrine and good actions: drowning evil in an abundance of good (cf. Rom 12: 21). That's how Christ will reign in our souls and in the souls of those around us."[29] To see God's image in others and to desire that they truly become Christ is the start and finish of what charity brings about, since charity is the salt, the essence, of a Christian's apostolate. "If it should lose its taste, how can we come to the world and proclaim: 'Here is Christ'?"[30]

---

[28] "You have a duty to reach those around you, to shake them out of their drowsiness, to open wide new horizons for their selfish, comfortable lives, to make their lives more *complicated* (in a holy way, that is), to help them forget about themselves and show understanding for others' problems. If not, you are not a good brother to your brothers in the human race. They need the *gaudium cum pace*, the peace and joy they have never known or have forgotten." *The Forge*, no. 900.

[29] *Christ Is Passing By*, no. 182.

[30] *Friends of God*, no. 234.

# PART TWO

# BEHAVIOR BEFITTING CHILDREN OF GOD

# CHAPTER 9

# Unity of Life for a Child of God

## The way things began

When God created the human race, he endowed it with a complex nature; harmony reigned among our natural powers, which were dominated by grace. This ensemble of gifts raised and perfected our nature, allowing us to aspire to the ultimate goal: intimate, eternal union with God.[1]

Thus, before sinning, man possessed, with sanctifying grace, all the gifts to make himself just in God's eyes: he was rightly related to God the Father as son and friend. United in friendship and harmony to his Creator, man effortlessly integrated both the natural and supernatural into a single entity, thanks to these preternatural gifts: *immortality*, whereby he could not die; *dominion* over the world and above all self-dominion, whereby he fully possessed himself; *freedom* from lusting after bodily pleasures, earthly goods, and excessive self sufficiency.

"Nevertheless, even so endowed, man found unity both a goal and task by reason of his freedom: God 'left him in the power of his own inclination' (Sir 15: 14). His essential unity as a person and the harmony—natural, supernatural, and preternatural—of all his operative powers arising from nature and grace were not enough. To them he was to add dynamic, existential unity by

---

[1] "The specific condition, both spiritual and material, of human nature presented a risk, even a threat or obstacle to the unity and perfect harmony of human life. That's why, St. Thomas Aquinas comments, God granted man 'the help of original justice, by virtue of which, if his mind submitted itself to God, the lesser corporeal powers would be wholly submissive to his will, allowing him to tend to God without impediment' (*Quaestiones disputatae. De Malo*, q. 5, a. 1, c). So strong was man's pristine harmony that neither his passions could fall into disorder nor his body separate itself from the soul and thus undergo corruption." I. Celaya, *Vivir como hijos de Dios*, 96–97.

freely and habitually choosing his only true and final end: glorifying God by knowing and loving his Creator."[2]

## Sin ruptured unity

Original sin was a failure for all mankind.[3] By rebelling against his God, his friend, and his father, man forfeited his integrity; his original innocence was lost. Till then, Adam and Eve had walked in the garden at dusk with their Father God; afterward they hid themselves out of fear (see Gen 3: 8). Breaking off friendship with God disrupted their entire lives. It generated internal struggles: shamefully they could no longer go naked, and so they devised garments. The rest of the natural world turned hostile, surrendering its yield only to toil. From that point forward human nature would experience fatigue, illness, birth pains, ignorance, and death.

From then on the original harmony had to be rebuilt by voluntary, virtuous efforts. "The world is good. Adam's sin destroyed the divine balance of creation; but God the Father sent his only Son to reestablish peace, so that we, his children by adoption, might free creation from disorder and reconcile all things to God."[4] This is the task and mission—our vocation amid the world—from God: to return all of creation to God by means of a personal unity of life.

"That is why I can tell you that our age needs to give back to matter and to the most trivial occurrences and situations their noble and original meaning. It needs to restore them to the service of God's kingdom, to spiritualize them, turning them into a means and occasion for a continual meeting with Jesus Christ."[5] Everything human, and therefore honest, can be made

[2] Ibid., 97.

[3] "The tree of the knowledge of good and evil symbolically evokes the outer limit that man as creature ought to recognize and respect. Man depends on his Creator; he finds himself subject to the laws upon which the Creator established the order of the universe created by him . . . consequently he also finds himself subject to the moral norms that regulate the use of his freedom." John Paul II, Address, September 3, 1986.

[4] *Christ Is Passing By*, no. 112.

[5] *Conversations with Monsignor Escrivá de Balaguer,* no. 114.

divine, even the most ordinary and unchallenging. "It is understandable that the Apostle should write: 'All things are yours, you are Christ's and Christ is God's' (1 Cor 3: 22–23). We have here an ascending movement which the Holy Spirit, infused in our hearts, wants to call forth from this world, upward from the earth to the glory of the Lord. And to make it clear that in that movement everything is included, even what seems most commonplace, St. Paul also wrote: 'In eating, in drinking, do everything as for the glory of God' (1 Cor 10: 31). . . . I assure you, my children, that when a Christian carries out with love the most insignificant everyday action, that action overflows with the transcendence of God."[6]

## Christ, the path to unity of life

Jesus, perfect God and perfect man, has reconciled earth with heaven, turning the slave into a child, while revealing to man his true identity. The path to divine filiation is the way to rebuild—by means of ascetical struggle in company with grace—our lives brought low by sin.

The need to cultivate a true unity of harmonic life (seeing oneself as a child of God always and everywhere) is indispensable to spiritual life. To follow Christ, we must orient all deeds toward him, thus identifying ourselves with him. Nothing is foreign or negligible to our Christian calling. Our interior struggle consists of the "task of bringing about unity of life, seconding grace."[7] Every instinct is shaped with love for God and neighbor.

We cannot forget that we wholly belong to God, and to him we direct our every endeavor, our rest, our healthy loves[8]. . . . At

[6] Ibid., nos. 115–116.

[7] I. Celaya, *Vivir como hijos de Dios*, 103: "At the outset, one must multiply ascetical practices that seem dispersed, but this seeming complication and addition—already linked by a common end—resolves itself into a higher unity. By growing in grace, the soul passes from the endeavor of adding to a superior unity embracing ever more. Then actions deemed at the start diverse are ever more permeated with charity. Eventually one no longer experiences them as separate."

[8] We can never overlook the danger of leading "a kind of double life. On one side, an interior life, a life of relation with God; and on the other, a separate and

our disposal is one single life, whose every deed should be for God.[9] There should not be times set aside for God and others for studying, working, earning a living: everything comes from God and should be done for him. In fact, unity of life is forged when in all our actions, however diverse and mundane, we try to seek God's glory, purifying our intentions and squeezing out the self-love and vanity our heart clings to. The subjective aim behind every deed (God's glory rather than personal ambition) is a prerequisite to unifying all our tasks. In sum: in our interior struggle we should strive to attain a strong unity of life, which leads us to identify our will with God's and thus to glorify him.

This path is undertaken when a soul "firmly and effectively decides to identify its will with God's. This gradual identification (the reverse of the disharmony wrought by sin) gradually integrates all our powers, which grow to the extent we ceaselessly seek God.

"Thus, unity of life coalesces around the growing desire behind every deed to recognize God as our ultimate end. This is what is meant by goodwill, giving man purity of intention.[10] Therefore, the nucleus of the Christian effort toward unity of life is simple and clear: to seek always and in all things only the love and glory of God."[11]

This quest begins with the morning offering: a Christian earmarks for God all the day's tasks, joys, and setbacks, everything.

---

distinct professional, social, and family life, full of earthly realities" (*Conversations*, no. 114). Vatican II warns us against this danger when it affirmed, "the divorce between faith and daily life, manifested by many people, ought to be viewed as one of the most serious mistakes of our age" (*Gaudium et spes*, no. 43).

[9] A life of prayer should pervade and transform the duties of every day. "Spirituality can never be seen as a sum of pious, ascetical practices, coexisting any which way with the rights and duties making up our walk in life. Rather, those very circumstances, if they represent God's will for us, are to be raised and supernaturally enlivened by a particular way of cultivating spiritual life, a growth to be reached amid and through those circumstances." Alvaro del Portillo, *Writings on the Priesthood*, 123.

[10] This was the perennial teaching of Blessed Josemaría: to achieve amid earthly chores a united life, which is, first and foremost, union with God; contemplative life, lending purpose to whatever is carried out.

[11] I. Celaya, *Vivir como hijos de Dios*, 104. See also *The Way*, no. 780.

At the outset the day is oriented to God, a renewable desire that nothing genuine be withdrawn from God's glory.[12]

## A single life

Striving each moment to be a child of God, the foundation of our integrated life, will largely take place at work, working hard and well for God; at home, enveloping it in peace and a spirit of service; and in friendship, the path whereby others are drawn more and more to God. In everything, at every moment of the day or night, we are to feed the desire to be, helped by grace, men and women of a single entity. We are not to be swayed by every passing breeze or to confine dealing with God to a pew at church or to times set aside for praying. Whether on the street, on the job, on the sports field, or at a social gathering, we have to be always the same: children of God who, with their affability and self-dominion, mirror what it means to follow Christ in the most diverse settings.[13] All earthly acts are to be lived through Christ—his grace is at the center of our soul—and ought to lead to him. This truth is what permits each task to be, at the same time, contemplation. Our personal sanctification is essentially tied to that of others. If we live in Christ, we shall look on the world as did he, with a merciful, winning gaze.

Here on earth one loves another creature at all hours of the day, not just at certain times. So too are we to learn how in

[12] Blessed Josemaría Escrivá used to say that we Christians have been empowered more than the legendary King Midas, who converted to gold all he touched. We are to convert into love for God, praising him, all our deeds, even the most trivial. See *The Forge*, no. 742.

[13] "So, whether you eat or drink, or whatever you do, do all to the glory of God" (1 Cor 10: 31), counseled the Apostle Paul to the first Christians.

In this regard St. Basil comments: "When you sit at the table, pray. When you eat bread, do so giving thanks to the all-generous One. If you drink wine, remember that it is granted to you for gladness and relieving illness. When you dress, give thanks to him who in his goodness gave it to you. When you gaze at the sky and the beautiful stars, throw yourself at God's feet and adore him who in his wisdom so wrought all things. Likewise, at dawn and dusk, whether asleep or awake, thank God who created and arranged all these things for your benefit, so that you might know, love, and praise the Creator." *Homilia in Julittam martirem* (PG 31–32).

spiritual life to discover how love for Christ constitutes the most intimate essence of our being. Thus does it shape our endeavors, whatever the circumstances: "In the world," said St. Augustine, "there are always bad days, but in God there are always good days." [14] Next to him, all days are good, despite both pain and failure.

By means of a united life, a Christian shows how Jesus is the source of light which illuminates every part of every day: family, work, business, friends, sickness, implementing the Church's social teachings in the various corners of life, caring for the environment (another gift from our Creator). . . . It does not make sense for a person intimate with God not to try meanwhile to be, as a result, cordial and optimistic, punctual and economical with time, a sworn enemy of shoddiness. . . . [15]

Professional chores, ordinary troubles, worries . . . all these are to feed our daily conversation with God. In turn, prayer ought to enrich all the circumstances we pass through. Alongside Christ, a Christian learns how to be a better friend, to live fully both justice and loyalty on the job, to be more human, to open and make oneself available to others in their needs. To achieve the unity of life that spells human and supernatural maturity, a Christian is to take many initiatives: to beg God's help in starting a task, to struggle to keep God present, to check for a pure intention. . . .

Love for God, if authentic, will be mirrored in all dimensions of life. We know now that temporal questions enjoy their own autonomy; there is no *Catholic solution* to social and political problems and so on. But neither do there exist pockets of neutrality, where a Christian can stop being and acting as such. When Christ is the purpose of one's whole life, a Christian works more and better. This is the strong thread—as with a string of fine pearls—that links all the deeds of the day. Then one avoids a double life: part for God and the rest for earthly

[14] *Commentaria in Psalmos* (PL 33:2, 17).

[15] "The unity of life of the lay faithful is most important. In effect they are to sanctify themselves in ordinary professional and social life. Therefore, to be able to correspond to their calling, the lay faithful ought to deem the activities of daily life as occasions for union with God and for fulfilling his will, as well as serving others, drawing them to communion with God in Christ." John Paul II, *Christifideles laici*, no. 17.

aims. A Christian's habitual objective and design should be to seek contemplative life amid everyday chores.

That is why in many ways Blessed Josemaría insisted: "We cannot lead a double life. We cannot be like schizophrenics if we want to be Christians. There is just one life, made of flesh and spirit. And it is this life that has to become, in both soul and body, holy and filled with God. We discover the invisible God in the most visible and material things." [16] A Christian is to recognize God's creative design for mankind as a *single life* made of flesh and spirit.

In a Christian's life, teaches Pope John Paul II, echoing the same strain, "there cannot be two parallel lives: on one hand, spiritual life with its values and demands; on the other, a so-called secular life, consisting of family life, work, social relations, political ties, culture. The branch rooted to the vine that is Christ is fruitful in each corner of his activity and existence. In effect, all the various fields of lay life enter into God's design, who desires them as the historical place where Christ's love makes itself present through the medium of Christians' lives. Every activity, every situation, every particular endeavor—such as professional competence and solidarity in one's work, love for and dedication to the family and educating children, social and political service, making the truth known in the cultural world—are providential occasions for 'a continuous exercise of faith, hope, and charity.' " [17] Thus does the desire to bring men to God and God to men flow forth wherever is found a disciple of Christ, for winning others stems directly from one's love for God and others.

---

[16] *Conversations with Monsignor Escrivá de Balaguer*, no. 114.

[17] John Paul II, *Christifideles laici*, no. 59; Vatican II, *Apostolicam actuositatem*, no. 4.

# CHAPTER 10

# The Freedom of God's Children

## True freedom found in God's will

Our freedom is not absolute, nor could it ever be. A limited being can enjoy only limited freedom. Moreover, true liberty "leads one to true goodness. The good in a person consists of being in the truth and carrying the truth out."[1] This gift of freedom, which the Creator granted to mankind, makes sense only when deployed in the name of man's quest for goodness and truth, for happiness. Just as colors and the paintbrush find their purpose in the painting, so is freedom aimed at human welfare. Only God is absolutely free. While God's free choice produces (creates) goodness, ours exists to discover goodness. In the possibility of choosing a means as an end (or a partial or only apparent good over an absolute good) is rooted our ability to sin. Sin is a disoriented choice, leading away from supreme goodness.

As an ultimate goal, man chooses either God or himself. There is no middle way, because only something absolute in itself, or wrongly deemed so, can be pursued as an ultimate end. St. Augustine expressed the dilemma in these terms: "Two loves founded two cities: love of self, to the extent of disdain for God, is the earthly love; love for God, to the exclusion of self, is the celestial. The former glories in itself; the latter, in God."[2] Let us not deceive ourselves. "Where there is no love for God, the individual and responsible use of personal freedom becomes impossible. There, despite appearances to the contrary, the individual is coerced at every turn."[3]

---

[1] John Paul II, *Veritatis splendor*, no. 84.

[2] *City of God*, book 14, c. 28 (PL 41:436).

[3] *Friends of God*, no. 29. "Our Holy Mother the Church has always spoken out in favor of freedom and has always rejected fatalism, both in its ancient and more modern versions. She has pointed out that each soul is master of its own destiny,

At some point in God's presence we might ask: "Lord, why have you given us this power? Why have you entrusted us with the faculty of choosing you or rejecting you? You want us to make good use of this power. Lord, what do you want me to do (see Acts 9: 6)? His reply is precise, crystal clear: 'You shall love the Lord your God with your whole heart and with your whole soul and with your whole mind' (Mt 22: 37)."[4] Here is God's design: the freedom to love him with all our spiritual might. "Freedom finds its true meaning when it is put to the service of the truth that redeems, when it is spent in seeking God's infinite love, which liberates us from all forms of slavery. Each passing day increases my yearning to proclaim to the four winds this inexhaustible treasure that belongs to Christianity: 'the glorious freedom of the children of God' (Rom 8: 21)! This is essentially what is meant by 'goodwill,' which teaches us to pursue 'good, after having distinguished it from evil.' "[5]

The predominant task of Christian life is to instruct and educate the will, so as to be guided ever more by God's will. Orientation to God should mark the path we follow, by means of resolutions and determinations taken conscientiously, in God's presence. Excluded therefore will be "I feel like it"; laziness; "what will others think!"; comfort; whatever seems at the time to be more useful or productive. . . . A child who draws ever closer to his Father, and grows therefore freer, will often ask himself: "What do you want from me, Lord, so that I may freely do it?"[6]

It was in this sense that St. Paul warned the first Christians not to use freedom as a cloak for malice: "For you were called to freedom, brethren; only do not use your freedom as an opportunity for the flesh" (Gal 5: 13). . . . St. Peter echoed these words: "Live as free men, yet without using your freedom as a pretext for evil; but live as servants of God" (1 Pet 2: 16). A child of God will not use something so precious as freedom to stray from the path.

---

for good or ill. . . . I have always been impressed by this awesome capacity which you and I have, which all of us have, a capacity that indeed reveals the nobility of our state." Ibid., no. 33.

[4] Ibid., no. 27.

[5] Ibid.; St. Maximus the Confessor, *Capita de caritate*, 2.32 (PG 90:995).

[6] *Friends of God*, no. 26.

A man can abuse his freedom if his definitive union with God is not confirmed by heaven. Meanwhile, the closer one gets to God, the greater attraction he feels for his end, and with it comes still greater freedom. The finest of saints more deeply crave holiness than others, while they enjoy greater freedom. The definitive and maximum possession of freedom comes with access to heaven.

Every good thing attracts the will, for goodness is its object. The closer one is to God, Supreme Goodness, the faster one tends in that direction in response to growing attraction. It is not unlike what happens gravitationally to iron filings in the face of an ever closer magnet.

But, when an attracted body reaches the ground (or the filings the magnet), they do not lose their attraction. Then it is at its greatest. Theirs is a definitively superior attraction, yet they cannot move. Analogously, saints in heaven are attracted by Supreme Goodness, possess freedom to the highest degree, yet they are irreversibly united to God. They thus enjoy eternal freedom; theirs is the restful possession of the Good they have long sought—the more so, the closer they got. That is why Blessed Josemaría asked: "Does our freedom vanish then? I assure you that it will then be more active than ever, because love is not content with a routine fulfillment of duty. Love is incompatible with boredom or apathy. To love means to renew our dedication every day, with loving deeds of service."[7] Freedom makes love new.

Opposed to freedom is coercion, not the rumination in search of Goodness. One cannot say, for example, that a mother has forfeited her freedom because, out of love for her children, she stays at home and declines going to the theater with her friends. Only in love is freedom fully realized.

## Our freedom won on the cross

Christian freedom is "the glorious liberty of the children of God" (Rom 8: 21), of those who serve their Father out of love. It is "for freedom Christ has set us free" (Gal 5: 1). Above all, it is

[7] Ibid., no. 31.

an inner reality for us, for it essentially consists in liberation from sin and in friendship with God (the only true choice).

Nothing hindered God from "creating us impeccable, irresistibly drawn toward the good. Nevertheless, 'he judged that his servants would be better if they served him freely.'[8] . . . Just think: the Almighty, who through his providence rules the whole universe, does not want the forced service of slaves; he prefers to have children who are free."[9]

The freedom of children—this is the freedom won by Christ for mankind. It is Christian freedom; that is, human freedom healed and raised by God's grace, the supernatural virtues, and the Holy Spirit's gifts. It is freedom without the ties and yoke that sin imposes on the will, thus hindering the quest for natural goods and closing the door to all supernatural goods. Christian freedom, therefore, is fruit of God's love, which makes us his children and guides us to him.[10]

A Christian who wants to be God's good child freely channels his life in one direction; he puts himself entirely at his Father's disposal, while aware that the paths God points out to his children are very different. In the depths of any Christian's soul should be the willingness to dedicate oneself unconditionally to God his Father. So will he habitually relate to God and love him. Such behavior, far from curtailing freedom, sees freedom increase. His is the experience of partaking of God's absolute freedom, of this God who is love, truth, and life.

[8] St. Augustine, *De vera religione*, 14.27 (PL 34:134).

[9] *Friends of God*, no. 33.

[10] Love for freedom will lead us "to defend the personal freedom of everyone, in the knowledge that 'Jesus Christ is the one who obtained that freedom for us' (Gal 4: 31). If we do not so behave, what right have we to claim our own freedom? We must also spread the truth, because *veritas liberabit vos* ('the truth will make you free': Jn 8: 32). The truth makes us free, while ignorance enslaves. We have to uphold the right of all men to live, to own what is necessary to lead a dignified existence, to work and to rest, to choose a particular state in life, to form a home, to bring children into the world within marriage and to be allowed to educate them, to pass peacefully through times of sickness and old age, to have access to culture, to join with other citizens to achieve legitimate ends, and, above all, the right to know and love God in perfect liberty, for conscience, true conscience, will discover the imprint of the Creator in all things." *Friends of God*, no. 171.

The decision to dedicate oneself, "binding" oneself out of love, ushers in new and greater freedom. "Only pride sees such bonds as a heavy chain. True humility, which is taught us by the One who is meek and humble of heart, shows that his yoke is easy and his burden light (see Mt 11: 29–30): his yoke is freedom and love and unity; his yoke is the life that Jesus won for us on the cross."[11]

A glance around us soon reveals that many bind, enslave, themselves to money, sensuality, power, work . . . even their health. "We will be slaves either way. Since we must serve anyway, for whether we like it or not this is our lot as men, then there is nothing better than recognizing that love has made us slaves of God. From the moment we recognize this, we cease being slaves and become friends, children."[12]

## Obedience and freedom of children

By virtuously obeying, we imitate Christ. He, "fulfilling his Father's will, inaugurated on earth the kingdom of heaven, revealed to us his mystery, and effected redemption, all through obedience."[13] St. Paul underscores Jesus' love for this virtue: being God, "he humbled himself and became obedient unto death, even death on a cross" (Phil 2: 8). The highest expression of his love for the Father's saving plans was to obey in dying, and the most ignominious of deaths, at that.

Love alone moved Christ to obey. There we have the key to the willing obedience of children of God: something we owe God and are to offer to the Church, parents, legitimate superiors, and in one way or another to social and professional peers. Jesus' obedience, as St. Paul teaches, consisted not in letting himself fall under the Father's will, but rather in expressly choosing to obey. His active obedience appropriated as his own

[11] Ibid., no. 31.

[12] Ibid., no. 35. "When we make up our minds to tell God, 'I put my freedom in your hands,' we find ourselves loosed from the many chains binding us to insignificant things, ridiculous cares, or petty ambitions. Then our freedom . . . will be used by us entirely to learn how to do good (see Is 1:17). This is the glorious freedom of children of God." Ibid., no. 38.

[13] Vatican II, *Lumen gentium*, no. 3.

the Father's designs and means to bring about the salvation of the human race. Therefore, the desire to obey is one of the best signs that one is treading the right path.[14] A Christian therefore should be on guard, since, the benefits of this virtue being so numerous, the devil in his crafty wiles will feed us false reasons and excuses not to obey. Without obedience, as St. Peter warns, freedom would become a "pretext for evil" (1 Pet 2: 16), to stray from the will of God. True obedience, on the other hand, is born of freedom and leads to ever greater freedom. When a man dedicates his will to obey, there remains to him the freedom of having chosen the good and true, God's will.[15]

Times of more acute struggle and temptations are excellent occasions for remembering what Scripture says, *Vir obediens loquetur victoriam*: "The obedient man will attain victory" (Prov 21: 28). "He who obeys, overcomes," Blessed Josemaría used to say. Such is given all the grace and light needed, because he receives the Holy Spirit, "given to those who obey him" (Acts 5: 32). "O virtue of obedience," exclaimed St. Teresa, "what can't you do?"[16]

Moreover, the need to obey comes not only from the benefits showered on our soul, but also from our intimate adherence to redemption. It is an essential part of the mystery of the cross and thus essential to our growth in holiness. That is why if someone were to put limits on what God asks of him, he would limit his union with Christ; hardly would he identify himself with Jesus, the end of all Christian life. "Have this mind among yourselves, which was in Christ Jesus, who, though he was in the form of God . . . emptied himself, taking the form of a servant . . . and became obedient unto death, even death on a cross" (Phil 2: 5–8). The Virgin Mary also sets an example of how to obey:

[14] Thomas Aquinas, *Commentary on the Epistle to the Philippians*, 2.8. St. Teresa of Avila used to say, "There is no more rapid path to perfection than that of obeying." *Foundations*, 5.10.

[15] "Obedience, far from being slavery, gives us the highest of freedom, the liberty of children of God, just as voluntary poverty obtains for us great spiritual riches, and by perfect chastity we are ushered into the intimacy of love." R. Garrigou-Lagrange, *The Three Ages of the Interior Life*, 2:713.

[16] *Life*, 18.7. Elsewhere she writes, "If ours is a pure conscience and obedience, God never permits the devil to deceive us to the extent of harming the soul; on the contrary, it's he who is deceived." *Foundations*, 4.2.

"Behold, I am the handmaid of the Lord; let it be to me according to your word" (Lk 1: 38). A soul that does not come to harbor a positive love for freedom, responsibility, and obedience, a love that will disclose their intimate connections, can scarcely hope to progress spiritually.

## Freedom and spiritual guidance

To act on freedom in Christian life requires discretion, that is, learning how to act and react with self-dominion, spontaneity, and Christian spirit, whatever the circumstances. True Christian men and women cannot be paralyzed in the face of the unexpected, nor do they need specific guidelines for unforeseen situations. Rather, they know how to seek solutions. Spiritual life is full of unanticipated events, which each is to meet with initiative, wisdom, and the aplomb born of doing the will of one's ever-loving Father God.

It is our responsible, dedicated freedom that brings forth virtues, allowing us to reach the maturity appropriate for an adult person seeking to orient his life toward his heavenly Father. "Freedom is the power, rooted in reason and will, to act or not to act, to do this or that, and so to perform deliberate actions on one's own responsibility. . . . [I]t attains its perfection when directed toward God, our beatitude."[17]

Stemming from the free and responsible commitment of children of God, Christians view what they receive in spiritual guidance, not as mandates, but as advice, guideposts. Consequently this counseling does not diminish their spontaneity or freedom, but rather suggests more possible initiatives.[18] This ad-

[17] *Catechism of the Catholic Church*, no. 1731. Spiritual guidance is aimed at removing the fear, if present, of acting on one's own, to make commitments, to be enterprising in one's own spiritual and apostolic life, in one's occupation, in sanctifying the family. "The more one does what is good, the freer one becomes . . . in the service of what is good and just." Ibid., no. 1733.

[18] Since they direct themselves to God freely, they cannot be marionettes who move in response to the pulling of strings; each must manage himself autonomously, with self-determination. "The task of spiritual guidance is not to bring forth creatures bereft of their own judgment and who only execute mechanically whatever they are told. On the contrary, spiritual guidance should aim at

vice is like the signs along the roads to help travelers reach their destination. We make them ours, lest we get lost; in no way do we view them as coercion. In fact, we are grateful for them, since they facilitate going directly to our goal. To follow Christ closely, a person pledges and commits himself, because he "simply wants to."[19] That is why one seeks out spiritual guidance, to compare his initiatives with God's will, to seek help and suggestions. And so, freely, he makes his own the directives received and struggles with greater conviction and effectiveness.

Apostolic efforts will also be full of the spontaneity and originality that come from the soul. One's whole life acquires the dominion born of full and responsible freedom.[20] Often the advice will be but the crowning of what one had already seen while praying: strengthen family life, be more generous in self-sacrifice, work more intensely, be more apostolically direct with one's friends. . . . The path to holiness calls for lots of initiatives.

Essentially, responsibility consists of being faithful to God's will, the supreme criterion to which all else must bend: "Do *what* pleases God and *how* it pleases him."[21] One is truly free and responsible only when seeking God's will in everything.

---

educating the faithful's conscience, supplying them with the criteria needed. To be such, they need maturity, firm convictions, adequate knowledge of doctrine, refinement of spirit, and a disciplined will." *Conversations with Monsignor Escrivá de Balaguer*, no. 93.

[19] Blessed Josemaría Escrivá used to express himself in these terms to indicate the decision to follow Christ with complete freedom. "I opt for God because I want to, freely, without compulsion of any kind. And I undertake to serve, to convert my whole life into a means of serving others, out of love for my Lord Jesus." *Friends of God*, no. 35. On another occasion he said, "Do things as God wants them done, *because we feel like it*, which is the most supernatural of reasons." *Christ Is Passing By*, no. 17.

[20] "Sanctity has the flexibility of supple muscles. Whoever wishes to be a saint should know how to behave so that while he does something that involves a mortification for him, he omits doing something else (as long as this does not offend God), which he also finds difficult, and thanks God for this comfort. If we Christians were to act otherwise we would run the risk of becoming stiff and lifeless, like a rag doll. Sanctity is not rigid like cardboard; it knows how to smile, to give way to others and to hope. It is life: a supernatural life." *The Forge*, no. 156.

[21] Benedict Baur, *In Silence with God*, 215.

"By itself . . . freedom is insufficient: it needs a guide, a pole-star."[22] And that can only be God's will, which expresses itself in many ways, a main one being through spiritual guidance. That is why those so educated highly esteem any further guidance.

[22] *Friends of God*, no. 26.

# CHAPTER 11

# Working As Children of God

## Work in God's original plan

A child of God is divinely called to sanctify himself amid the secular world. For that he must be closely united to Jesus, so as to be able, with him, from him, and through him, to convert into expressions of love all he undertakes. Blessed Josemaría used to say: "You have received God's call to a specific way: it is to be at all the crossroads of the world, while remaining all the while, and as you carry out your professional work, in God."[1] "In God," "godliness," "intimate with God" . . . these expressions point to the fundamental reality: to be and to conduct oneself as God's child in any circumstance, not least in one's work.

Throughout history work has been seen as punishment, but that does not need to be so.[2] Man perfects himself in fulfilling God's design of cooperating with his Father both in creation and in divine providence: maintaining and caring for everything. Work is not a penal sentence. The punishment for the primal sin was the loss of friendship with God and, with it, exemption from death, suffering, ignorance, loss of bodily and earthly dominion, fatigue. When the Word came into history, he restored us to God's friendship. He also has energized us so that we can overcome these disorders. So, now work too has a new meaning.

By taking it upon himself as part of his life at Nazareth, Jesus redeemed work and made it redemptive. Work, therefore, is a good, a great good, without which one could hardly strive for

---

[1] *The Forge*, no. 748.

[2] On the contrary, "work is man's original vocation. It is a blessing from God, and those who consider it a punishment are sadly mistaken. The Lord, who is the best of fathers, placed the first man in paradise *ut operaretur:* so that he would work" (*Furrow*, no. 482). And all that *before* original sin.

human completion. "Work is part and parcel of man's life on earth. It involves effort, weariness, exhaustion: signs of the suffering and struggle accompanying human existence and that point to the reality of sin and the need for redemption. But in itself work is not a penalty or curse or punishment. Those who speak of it that way have not understood sacred Scripture properly. . . . Work, all work, bears witness to man's dignity, to his dominion over creation. It is an opportunity to develop one's personality. It is a bond of union with others, the way to support one's family, a means of aiding in the improvement of the society in which we live and in the progress of all humanity.

"For a Christian these horizons extend and grow wider. For work is a participation in God's creative work. When he created man and blessed him, he said: 'Be fruitful, multiply, fill the earth, and conquer it. Be masters of the fish of the sea, the birds of heaven, and all living animals on the earth' (Gen 1: 28). And, moreover, since Christ took it into his hands, work has become for us a redeemed and redemptive reality. Not only is it the background of man's life, it is a means and path of holiness."[3] God himself, in the Person of the Word, has bent down to our level, becoming one of us. There God's children ground their love for the world and work.[4]

Children of God work very differently from those unaware of that dignity. The latter give the impression of being saddled with an unavoidable evil. A child of God, however, perfects creation; he works at home, at the home of his Father God, the world over. Any honest task can improve whoever carries it out, not to mention society itself; plus it can help others by means of the Communion of Saints. For that one cannot forget both the supernatural and human value that can and ought to be discovered in each and every daily deed, even the hardest and most trying. "Galley slaves, for example, certainly know they are rowing to propel the ship; but to recognize that this rowing can give meaning to their existence, they will have to delve into the Christian significance of suffering and expiation. In other

[3] *Christ Is Passing By*, no. 47.

[4] "The Lord wants his children, those of us who have received the gift of faith, to proclaim the original optimistic view of creation, the *love for the world* that is the heart of the Christian message. So there should always be enthusiasm in your professional work and in your effort to build up the earthly city." *The Forge*, no. 703.

words, they will have to understand their situation as an opportunity for identification with Christ. Otherwise, they will hate their work. A similar difficulty arises when the fruit of one's labor (not the wage, but the product made) is completely removed from one's ken [at the end of a long production chain]."[5]

Unfortunately, how many go to work each morning as if reporting to the galley! There they indifferently row for a ship whose destination is unknown. Their only hope is for weekends and their paycheck. Working so, obviously, does not dignify or sanctify; barely will it benefit one's personality or society itself. But that cannot be the case for a child of God.

## How Christ toiled

All of Jesus' doings were works of God, something he deified. How telling that "of Jesus' thirty-three years, thirty were spent in silence and obscurity, submission and work."[6] No wonder some of his neighbors said to him, "Leave here and go to Judea, that your disciples may see the works you are doing. For no man works in secret if he seeks to be known openly" (Jn 7: 3–4).

Daily chores are something rich in promise, which children of God are to discover. No one can imitate Christ without a life overflowing with work. "I don't understand how you can call yourself a Christian and lead such an idle, useless life. Have you forgotten Christ's life of toil?"[7]

God chose for himself a simple occupation so as to help us understand that it is love for God that gives meaning to our deeds.[8] The value of Christ's deeds was always infinite. He gave the same glory to his Father when he was nailed to the cross,

[5] Peter Berglar, *Opus Dei*, 256–257.

[6] *Furrow*, no. 485.

[7] *The Way*, no. 356.

[8] "Our Lord, perfect man in every way, chose a manual trade and carried it out attentively and lovingly for almost the entirety of the years he spent on earth. He worked as a craftsman among the other people in his village. This human and divine activity of his shows us clearly that our ordinary activities are not an insignificant matter. Rather they are the very hinge on which our sanctity turns, and they offer us constant opportunities of meeting God and of praising and glorifying him through our intellectual or manual work." *Friends of God*, no. 81.

when he restored to life a dead person, or when he was followed by crowds praising God. Like the other men in Nazareth, Jesus worked. He did not differ from them, for he was one of them. And we cannot forget that the temporal existence of God's Son was made up of both his public and hidden life.

When Jesus returns later to Nazareth, the village dwellers are surprised by his wisdom and astonished at the feats told of him. He is known by his craft and as "Mary's son." "Where did this man get all this? . . . Is not this the carpenter, the son of Mary?" (Mk 6: 2–3). St. Matthew also tells us, on another occasion, what people thought of Jesus: "Is not this the carpenter's son? Is not his mother called Mary?" (13: 55). For years on end, day after day, they saw him busy in his shop. No wonder he was known by his job.

Moreover, Christ's preaching hints that he was well acquainted with the world of work. He often draws examples from his personal experiences. In the Nazareth years of hidden life, Christ is teaching us the value of ordinary life as a means to holiness. "Man's ordinary life among his fellows is not something dull and uninteresting. It is there that God wants the vast majority of his children to achieve sanctity."[9] Christ's job was neither easy nor outstanding; nor did it promise much. But Jesus loved his daily work, and he taught us to love ours. Otherwise we cannot hope to sanctify it.

Jesus was no stranger to the tiredness and fatigue of physical labor. He too experienced the monotony of days with no apparent relief or impact. This realization can be very beneficial to us. "The sweat and tiredness that work necessarily entails in the current condition of mankind, offer a Christian, and anyone else for that matter, both called to follow Christ, the possibility of partaking of the love for the work Christ came to carry out. This work of salvation was wrought by the very means of suffering and death on the cross. Enduring work's fatigue in union with Christ crucified for us, man collaborates in a certain way with the Son of God in redeeming mankind. He shows himself to be Jesus' true disciple, bearing in his turn the cross of every day by doing what he has been called to do."[10]

---

[9] *Christ Is Passing By*, no. 110.
[10] John Paul II, *Laborem exercens*, no. 27.

During those thirty unobtrusive years, Jesus is the model to imitate in our role as ordinary working people. Imaginatively reconstructing how he toiled in his workshop, we will understand better our duty to fulfill our obligations conscientiously. It makes no sense to try to hallow sloppy work. We are to learn to find God in our daily occupations, to help our fellow citizens, and to raise to new heights both society and all creation.[11] Those who seek to identify themselves with Christ must work well, work hard, and never stop learning.

## Finding our Father at work

With Christ everything human can be divine. "Your work too must become a personal prayer, a real conversation with our Father in heaven."[12] A Christian's vocation requires our carrying out our role in the thick of society. "Your human vocation is a part—an important part—of your divine vocation. That is the reason why you must strive for holiness, giving a particular character to your human personality, a style to your life; contributing at the same time to the sanctification of others, your peers; sanctifying your work and the environment: the profession or job that fills your day, your home and family, and the country where you were born and that you love."[13]

A housewife dedicated to her children and to God becomes a domestic expert, administering well both money and schedules. She is also to make the house attractive, tastefully decorated, so that her family takes pride in it. She knows her husband and children well and, if necessary, will point out to them individually where they might improve—and all this in a simple, loving way. She will know how to manage all responsibilities professionally, establishing priorities and a schedule, being efficient but not neglecting small details, skipping a meal when duty calls. Likewise, to be a good Christian, a student is to be an achiever, alert in classes, keeping up with the various courses, taking good notes, doing homework punctually. Equally competent are to be the

---

[11] See Vatican II, *Lumen gentium*, no. 41.

[12] *Friends of God*, no. 64.

[13] *Christ Is Passing By*, no. 46.

architect, the secretary, the fashion designer, the businessman. . . . "A Christian who neglects his temporal duties," says Vatican II, "defrauds his neighbors and, above all, ignores his obligations to God and may even endanger his eternal salvation."[14] Such negligence in something so essential is a big mistake and, if not mended, makes it impossible to be God's good child. With our daily tasks we are to scale heaven. Thus we are to imitate Jesus, "who endowed labor with a preeminent dignity, working with his own hands."[15]

To emulate our Lord, "we have to be contemplative souls in the midst of the world, who try to convert their work into prayer." [16] These words disclose the core of Christian toil. Whatever a child of God does is to be transformed, converted into prayer. As Pope John Paul II reminds us, the history of mankind knows no person who, so fully and exquisitely, dwelled on God in prayer as Jesus of Nazareth. Prayer was the very life of his soul, and all this life was prayer.[17] His soul's life was love. What, therefore, can convert labor into prayer? God's Love personified: the Holy Spirit in the hearts of God's children. He shapes the soul to identify it with Christ; he transforms work into divine dialogue. He who makes us children of God raises our work to God in union with him. One can consequently say that "work is born of love; it is a manifestation of love and is directed toward love." [18] God's children toil out of love, with their work they show their love, and their work as God's children is oriented to (for such is to pray) love. Work is made holy when, with an upright intention, it is directed to God, because one brings to it a supernatural aim, besides honest human purposes.[19]

Therefore, when we raise everything to our Father God, "there is no human undertaking that cannot be sanctified, that cannot be an opportunity to sanctify ourselves and to cooperate with God in the sanctification of the people with whom we

[14] *Gaudium et spes*, no. 43.

[15] Ibid., no. 67.

[16] *Furrow*, no. 497.

[17] Address, July 22, 1987.

[18] *Christ Is Passing By*, no. 48.

[19] See *The Way*, no. 359. Then work is "prayer and thanksgiving, because we know we are placed on earth by God, that we are loved by him and made heirs to his promises." *Christ Is Passing By*, no. 48.

work. The light of Jesus Christ's followers should not be hidden in the depths of some valley, but should be placed on the mountain peak, so that 'they may see your good works and give glory to your Father in heaven' (Mt 5: 16).

"To work in this way is to pray. To study thus is likewise prayer. Research done with this spirit is prayer too. We are always doing the same thing, for everything can be prayer, all activity can and should lead us to God, nourish our intimate dealings with him, from morning to night. Any honorable work can be prayer, and all prayerful work is apostolic. In this way the soul develops an integrated life, which is both simple and strong." [20] Then one beholds the harmony of Christian life, the unity of life lost by sin and recovered in Christ.

Thus, little by little, children of God learn to be contemplatives in the world: "in the midst of the din of the throng, know how to find silence of soul in a lasting conversation with our Lord, people who know how to look at him as they look at a father, as they look at a friend, as they look at someone with whom they are madly in love." [21] Nonetheless, just because such dialogue is possible does not make it easy. But then neither did arithmetic come easy at the start, but by doing drills over and over again, while corrected by the teacher, they become second nature.

We are garden-variety Christians, "who habitually find themselves in the hubbub of the city, in the light of day, in the street, at work, with their families, or simply relaxing, but centered on Jesus all day long. . . . At first it will be more difficult. You must make an effort to seek out the Lord, to thank him for his fatherly and practical concern for us. Although it is not a question of sentiment, little by little God's love makes itself felt like a rustle in the soul. It is Christ who pursues us lovingly: 'Behold, I stand at the door and knock' (Rev 3: 20)." [22] It may be harder at the start, and maybe later also. It is crucial to be consistent in our efforts to direct our chores to God by building up the habit of God's presence.

Labor is converted by God's Love who dwells in our praying

[20] *Christ Is Passing By*, no. 10.
[21] *The Forge*, no. 738.
[22] *Christ Is Passing By*, no. 8.

hearts and unites them to our heavenly Father, wherever we may be.

## Working in our Father's home

Our love for the world is born of our being children, not slaves; owners, not hired hands. Thus, "amid the limitations accompanying our present life, where sin is still present in us to some extent . . . we Christians perceive with particular clearness all the wealth of our divine filiation, when we realize that we are fully free because we are doing our Father's work, when our joy becomes constant, because no one can take our hope away."[23] Each day our Father God tells us, "Son, go and work in the vineyard today" (Mt 21: 28).

Faithful children serving their Father: that is how we are to see ourselves. At work, at home, they know how at every turn to do as their Father would. Then, "in the most varied activities of our day, in all situations, we must act as God's servants, realizing that he is with us, that we are his children. We must be aware of the divine roots burrowing into our life and act accordingly."[24]

To do so, let us keep before our eyes the Model who pleased his Father God. "He has done all things well," we read in Mark (7: 37). Thus, let us try to work hard and well. "It's no good offering to God something that is less perfect than our poor human limitations permit. The work that we offer must be without blemish and it must be done as carefully as possible, even in the smallest details, for God will not accept shoddy workmanship. 'You shall not offer anything that is faulty' (Lev 22: 20). . . . For that reason, the work of each of us, the activities that take up our time and energy, must be an offering worthy of our Creator. It must be *operatio Dei,* a work of God that is done for God: in short, a task that is complete and faultless."[25]

The owner of a business never thinks he is devoting too much time to it. An employee, on the other hand, may think he

[23] Ibid., no. 138.
[24] Ibid., no. 60.
[25] *Friends of God*, no. 55.

has too much to do, when in fact, what little he has is done routinely. In the face of abundant chores, children of God neither quit nor slack off. Generosity comes easily when facing with Christ the prospect of bringing redemption to the world. The desire to imitate Christ pushes a Christian not only to fulfill his work lovingly, with a dialogue that need never end, but also to see somehow as his own others' tasks, since they are things belonging to his Father God. That is why Blessed Josemaría wrote: "When you have finished your work, do your brother's, helping him, for the sake of Christ, with such finesse and naturalness that no one—not even he—will realize that you are doing more than what in justice you ought. This, indeed, is virtue befitting a child of God!" [26]

[26] *The Way*, no. 440.

# CHAPTER 12

# How Children of God Pray

## Childlike piety

While many persons try to find their way to God, we Christians know especially well that he is our Father, untiringly watching over us. "The expression 'God the Father' had not been revealed to anyone. Moses himself, when he asked God who he was, received another name. But to us the name has been revealed by the Son."[1] Every time we turn to him, we hear, "Son, you are always with me, and all that is mine is yours" (Lk 15: 31). None of our needs or sadnesses goes unnoticed by him. If we start to fall, he hurries to support us or to raise us up.[2]

Prompted by divine filiation, life acquires a new meaning. No longer a mystery to be solved, life is a task to be carried out in our Father's home, all of creation. If we constantly see ourselves as such, we will become men and women of prayer. And how does a child deal with his father, except with respect, veneration, consideration, and love. "Piety born of divine filiation is a profound attitude of soul that eventually permeates one's entire existence. It is there in every thought, every desire, every affection."[3]

---

[1] Tertullian, *Treatise on Prayer*, CSEL 20:180-200, 3.

[2] He "is a Father who is full of tenderness, of infinite love. Call him 'Father' many times a day and tell him—alone, in your hearts—that you love him, that you adore him, that you feel proud and strong because you are his child. All this implies a genuine program of interior life, which needs to be channeled through your relationship of piety with God, through these acts (which should be few, I insist, but constant), which will enable you to develop the attitudes and manners of a good child." *Friends of God*, no. 150.

[3] Ibid., no. 146.

# Jesus' prayer as Son

Babies come into the world with a capacity to eventually speak or, at least, with the possibility of communicating with others with smiling, crying, eye contact, and so on. Later on they produce sounds unintelligible to all, except their mother. Learning to speak is a mystery of love, repeating itself over and over again. The child learns his first syllables and then his first words. Almost always and everywhere, regardless of tongue, the first full word is "Daddy." Behind lies the loving desire of acquainting the child with his father, a lesson strengthened by the example of his sisters and brothers. A Christian, taught by his mother Mary, learns over time how to speak, the gestures, the responses, the way of being, the sentiments of his other brother, Christ, the exact image of the Father. A child of God needs to dialogue with his Father at all times. And it is Jesus Christ, the first-born, who teaches us to call on him as Father: "No one comes to the Father, but by me" (Jn 14: 6).[4]

He "learned to pray in his human heart. He learns to pray from his mother, who kept all the great things the Almighty had done and treasured them in her heart (see Lk 1: 49; 2: 19; 2: 51). He learns to pray in the words and rhythms of the prayer of his people, in the synagogue at Nazareth and the Temple at Jerusalem. But his prayer springs from an otherwise secret source, as he declares at the age of twelve: 'I must be in my Father's house' (Lk 2: 49). Here the newness of prayer in the fullness of time begins to be revealed: his *filial prayer*, which the Father awaits from his children, is finally going to be lived out by the only Son in his humanity, with and for men." [5]

Jesus teaches us this "secret source" from which springs his prayer: familiarity with our Father God. The Gospels show him, on many occasions, withdrawing from the crowds to unite himself with his Father in prayer (see Mt 14: 23; Lk 6: 12). From

---

[4] "Those we love figure constantly in our conversations, desires, and thoughts. We hold them ever present. So it should be with God. When we so seek our Lord in this way, our whole day becomes one intimate and trusting conversation with him. . . . [O]ur Lord has shown us by his example that this is exactly what we have to do: we have to pray at all times, from morning to night and from night to morning." Ibid., no. 247.

[5] *Catechism of the Catholic Church*, no. 2599.

him we learn the need to dedicate some time exclusively to God amid our daily rounds. At special times he prays for the mission he is to carry out; then his prayer is one of filial abandonment to the Father's will, such as in Gethsemani and on Calvary (see Mk 14: 35–36; Mk 15: 34; Lk 23: 44–46). On other occasions he prays trustingly for others, especially for the apostles and their subsequent disciples, for us (see Lk 22: 32; Jn 17). In many ways he teaches us that this childlike, confident intimacy with God is needed to resist temptation (see Mt 26: 41), to obtain what we need (see Jn 4: 10; 6: 27), and to persevere to the end (see Lk 21: 36).

This childlike conversation ought to be personal, behind a closed door, "in secret" (Mt 6: 5–6). Thus is it to be uncomplicated (see Mt 6: 7–8), humble, like the publican's (see Lk 18: 9–14); constant and unflagging, like the inopportune friend or the widow pestering the judge (see Lk 11: 5–8; 18: 1–8); steeped in trust in God's goodness (see Mk 11: 23). For God knows the needs of his children and gives them not only goods for their soul but also for their physical life (see Mt 7: 7–11; Lk 11: 9–13).

Often did Jesus go off alone and pray at length—sometimes for whole nights. Thus one day, when he was finishing his prayer, his disciples asked the Master in all simplicity: "teach us to pray" (Lk 11: 1–4). From Jesus' lips they learned the Our Father, words to be on millions of lips, in all tongues, and thus they were taught a completely new way of relating to God.

"We can relive the scene when Jesus retires to pray and his disciples are nearby, probably watching him. When Jesus has finished, one of them boldly asks him: 'Lord, teach us how to pray, as John did for his disciples.' And he told them, 'When you pray, you are to say, "Father, hallowed be your name"' (Lk 11: 1–2).

"Note the surprising thing about this reply. The disciples share their daily lives with Jesus and there, in the course of their ordinary conversations, our Lord tells them how they should pray. He reveals to them the great secret of God's mercy: that we are children of God and can talk things over with him and spend time with him, just as trustingly as a child does with a parent."[6] Christ shows us how to deal with God as our Father and how

---

[6] *Friends of God*, no. 145.

we are to ask for help. He is the Way leading to the summit of prayer, ushering us into divine intimacy.

The very first word Christ instructs us to pronounce is *Father.* The first Christians kept the word *Abba* in Aramaic, which Jesus used; it is very probable that that is why it entered into the oldest liturgy of the Church.[7] This first word sets the tone of confidence and filiation that should always characterize our turning to God. The Lord chose to avoid certain words, teaches the *Roman Catechism*, "that could cause fear in us and only employed one that would inspire love and trust in those who pray and ask for something. What could be more pleasing than the name of *Father*, which implies tenderness and love?"[8] The word *Abba* that Jesus used is the same as that used by Hebrew children when they familiarly and affectionately call upon their earthly parents. And this was the word chosen by Jesus as the most appropriate in calling upon the Creator of the world: Abba, Daddy!

The same God who transcends creation is yet very close to us. He is a Father tightly linked to the existence of his children, however weak and ungrateful; he only desires us to be with him for all eternity. We have been born for heaven.

## Perseverance

Christ leads us by the hand to the Father; he teaches us how to deal with him and in what words. "My advice is that, in your prayer, you actually take part in the different scenes of the Gospel, as one more among the people present. First of all, imagine the scene or mystery you have chosen to help you recollect your thoughts and meditate. Next, apply your mind, concentrating on the particular aspect of the Master's life you are considering—his merciful heart, his humility, his purity, the way he fulfills his Father's will. Then tell him what happens to you in these matters, how things are with you, what is going on in your soul. Be attentive, because he may want to point something out to you, and you will experience suggestions deep in your soul, realizing certain things and feeling his gentle reprimands."[9]

---

[7] Cf. W. Marchel, *Abbá, Père. La prière du Christ et des chrétiens,* 188–189.

[8] IV, 9, 1.

[9] *Friends of God,* no. 253

Ordinarily, parents prefer letters over phone calls from their children, since the former can be read and reread, even between the lines. Thus they might discover how their children are getting on, whether they need something they do not want to trouble their parents about. . . . But parents do discover them, thanks to lovingly reading their letters. Well, the same thing happens in spiritual life. "In the interior life, as in human love, we have to persevere.

"You have to meditate often on the same themes, keeping it up till you *rediscover* an old discovery. 'How could I not have seen this so clearly before?' you'll ask in surprise. Simply because sometimes we're like stones, which let the water flow over them, without absorbing a drop. That's why we have to go over the same things again and again—because they aren't the same things—if we want to soak up God's blessings." [10] And so, one good day, after having heard it and considered it so very often, you'll say: God is my Father! And, by meditating on it again, assures Blessed Josemaría, "You will never let go of this consoling thought. Jesus is my dear Friend (another thrilling discovery), who loves me with all the divine madness of his heart.

"The Holy Spirit is my Consoler, who guides my every step along the road. Consider this often: you are God's—and God is yours." [11]

Let us not grow tired of mulling over the same things until we "get it." Little children, to the degree they learn to talk and their minds begin to grow, start speaking up in conversations with their parents. They come to grasp intimate reasons why the family does this or that; they become tactful; they volunteer and try to console, rather than to be consoled. This is echoed in the spiritual life, so that "whenever we feel in our hearts a desire to improve, a desire to respond more generously to our Lord, and we look for something to guide us, a north star to guide our lives as Christians, the Holy Spirit will remind us of the words of the Gospel that we 'ought to pray continually and never be discouraged' (Lk 18: 1). Prayer is the foundation of any supernatural endeavor. With prayer we are all-powerful; without it, if we were to neglect it, we would accomplish nothing." [12]

[10] *The Forge*, no. 540.
[11] Ibid., no. 2.
[12] *Friends of God*, no. 238.

Children, especially when young and innocent, often repeat themselves. Our Father God never tires of our insistence. Thus, like them, we should know that "those who are nearest are the first to be heard. That is why you must get close to God and be intent on becoming a saint."[13] Taking a cue from children, let us be insistent when making our requests of God. A little one gets what he wants from his father by stubbornly insisting—that is the way we should pray.

## A child with his father

Divine filiation, viewing oneself as a child of God, is what defines a Christian's prayer, a dialogue ever more flowing and unrestrained. It is how a friend talks with a friend, the way a tot speaks with his father, confiding in him one's sufferings and joys, one's needs and fears.[14]

"How should we pray? I would go as far as to say, without fear of being mistaken, that there are many, countless, ways of praying. But I would like all of us to pray genuinely, as God's children, not gabbing away like hypocrites who will hear from Jesus' lips 'Not everyone who says to me, "Lord, Lord!" shall enter into the kingdom of heaven' (Mt 7: 21). People who live by hypocrisy can perhaps achieve 'the sound of prayer,' says St. Augustine, 'but they cannot possess its voice, because there is no life in them.'[15] They lack the desire to fulfill the Father's will. When we cry 'Lord!' we must do so with an effective desire to put into practice the inspirations the Holy Spirit awakens in our soul.

"We must strive to eliminate any shadow of deceit on our part. If we are to banish this evil, which Jesus condemned so severely, we must first try to ensure that our dispositions, both

[13] *Furrow*, no. 648.

[14] "Over the years I have sought to rely unfalteringly for my support on this joyous reality. No matter what the situation, my prayer, while varying in tone, has always been the same. I have said to him: 'Lord, you put me here. You entrusted me with this or that, and I put my trust in you. I know you are my Father, and I have seen that tiny children are always absolutely sure of their parents.' " *Friends of God*, no. 143.

[15] *Enarrationes in Psalmos*, 139.10 (PL 37:1809).

habitual and actual, are those of a clear aversion to sin."[16] Sincerity in prayer, in conversing with God, implies not wanting to wrong him, not even venially. It is the first step to true praying.

The dialogue ordinarily begins with repeated, short phrases, however insignificant. "First, one brief aspiration, then another, and another . . . till our fervor seems insufficient, because words are too poor . . . then this gives way to intimacy with God, looking at God without needing rest or feeling tired."[17]

Nevertheless, we would be deceiving ourselves if we were to think that prayer is easy or that sentiment always accompanies good desires. "I don't mind telling you that the Lord has, on occasion, given me many graces. But as a rule I have to go against the grain."[18] Elsewhere Blessed Josemaría points out: "Remember that prayer does not consist in making pretty speeches or high-sounding, consoling phrases.

"Prayer, at times, will be a glance at a picture of our Lord or of his Mother; sometimes a petition, expressed in words; or offering good works and the fruits of faithfulness. We have to be like a guard on sentry duty at the gate of God our Lord: that's what prayer is. Or like a small dog that lies down at his master's feet. Do not mind telling him: Lord, here I am, like a faithful dog; or better still like a little donkey, which will not kick the one who loves him."[19]

So often in ordinary life little children have to put on some act for visitors. And things can easily go wrong, perhaps embarrassing their parents, not because the child disobeys but rather because he gets nervous "with an audience." The same thing can happen to us in our dealings with God. That's why Blessed Josemaría affirmed, "I do not deny that over the years people have come to me and have told me with real sorrow: 'Father, I don't know what's come over me, but I find I am tired and cold. My piety used to be so solid and straightforward, but now it feels like play acting'. . . . Well, for those going through such a phase and for all of you, I answer: 'Play acting? Wonderful! God is playing with us as a father does with his children.'

[16] *Friends of God*, no. 243.
[17] Ibid., no. 296.
[18] Ibid., no. 152.
[19] *The Forge*, no. 73.

"We read in Scripture: 'God plays over the whole face of the earth.' But he does not abandon us because he adds immediately, 'My delight is to be with the children of men' (Prov 8: 31). God is playing with us! So when we feel that we are just play acting, because we feel cold and uninspired; when we find it difficult to fulfill our duties and attain the spiritual objectives we had set ourselves, then the time has come for us to realize that God is playing with us, and that he wishes us to act out our *play* with style."[20]

## Personal prayer

Prayer is indispensable for us; if we neglect conversing with God, our spiritual life shrivels up little by little. "If you abandon prayer you may at first live on spiritual reserves, and after that, by cheating."[21] On the other hand, prayer unites us to God, who tells us, "Apart from me you can do nothing" (Jn 15: 5). Let us keep on praying and not lose heart (see Lk 18: 1). We are to speak with him and draw close to him in all settings of our life: "Without prayer, how difficult it is to accompany him!"[22]

Jesus teaches us with the example of his life what our attitude is to be: a filial dialogue with God.[23] This dialogue should not be interrupted; it is to continue amid all our undertakings. But this closeness must be more thorough in the times we reserve for mental prayer: meditating and speaking in his presence, truly knowing that he *hears and sees us*. To go forward on the path to holiness, especially when we are weighed down by our frailty, let us recollect ourselves in prayer, in intimate conversation with our heavenly Father.

Prayer overflows in warmth and strength: an apostolic fire that burns and purifies. "That's why you go to prayer: to become a blaze, a living flame giving heat and light."[24] "Now as

---

[20] *Friends of God*, no. 152.

[21] *Furrow*, no. 445.

[22] *The Way*, no. 89.

[23] "In my view mental prayer is nothing more than friendly dealings, trying many times to be alone with One whom we know loves us." St. Teresa of Avila, *Life*, 8.2.

[24] *The Way*, no. 92.

you pray, you realize that this is the source that wells up within true children of God." [25]

Public prayer is holy and necessary, for God wants to see his children praying together (see Mt 18: 19–20). But also necessary is our intimate dialogue with God. The liturgy is public prayer *par excellence*: "It is the peak toward which tends all the Church's activity and from which flows all its strength." [26] Yet "spiritual life cannot be content with just participating in the sacred liturgy. While a Christian is called to pray in common, nevertheless he ought also to go into his room and pray to his Father in secret. Even more, according to the Apostle, he is to pray without ceasing (see 1 Thess 5: 17)." [27] Prayer in common with other Christians can also be personal prayer, provided the recitation accommodates pauses and the mind tries its best to concentrate.

Personal prayer involves speaking with God much as one would converse with a friend, knowing him to be present, ever attentive to what we say, listening to and answering us. This intimate colloquy is where we open our heart to God, to adore, thank, seek strength, and to plumb, like the apostles, divine teachings. [28] Ours can never be impersonal, anonymous prayer. It is to be a dialogue of a specific person—who has a goal and an occupation, and certain friends . . . and specific graces from God—with his heavenly Father.

Often we will have to turn to the Gospels or some other book to spur this dialogue, as did the saints. St. Teresa confides, "Unless just after communion, I never dared to start praying without a book. My soul feared to do without it as much as it would be scared to fight single-handedly against an angry crowd. With its help, something like a platoon or shield to absorb the blows arising from many helter-skelter thoughts, I was consoled." [29]

[25] *Furrow*, no. 455.

[26] Vatican II, *Sacrosanctum Concilium*, no. 10.

[27] Ibid., no. 12.

[28] "You wrote to me, 'To pray is to talk with God. But about what?' About what? About him, about yourself: joys, sorrows, successes and failures, great ambitions, daily worries—even your weaknesses! And acts of thanksgiving and petitions, and love and reparation. In short: to get to know him and to get to know yourself—to 'get acquainted'!" *The Way*, no. 91.

[29] *Life*, 6.3.

Let us use the means to pray mentally with recollection. That means the best place and time according to our circumstances; whenever possible, next to our Lord in the tabernacle. While praying, we should fend off distractions, largely by means of quieting the imagination and memory, so that we will not be hindered in attending to God. Avoid keeping "your senses awake and your soul asleep." [30]

If we struggle decisively against distractions, God will help us return to dialoguing with him. Moreover, our guardian angels are charged with interceding for us. What is crucial is not willingly wanting to be distracted. Involuntary distractions, despite our efforts to rid ourselves of them when we become aware of them, diminish neither the benefit nor the merit of our prayer. Are parents angry when their baby mutters incoherent sounds? God not only knows our weakness but is supremely patient. What is key is to ask him for help.

How pleased God is with our resolve to better our mental prayer even when we must strain against blankness and aridity. "Prayer is not a question of what you say or feel, but of love. And you love when you try hard to say something to the Lord, even though you might not actually say anything." [31] If we thus try, our whole life will be enriched and strengthened. Prayer is a powerful beacon to help us see problems better, to know others more so as to be able to help them on their way to Christ, to gain perspective with regard to things that worry us. Prayer leaves an atmosphere of peace and serenity in the soul that we cannot keep to ourselves. Its joy is a foretaste of the bliss awaiting us in heaven.

On earth no one knew better how to deal with Jesus than his Mother, who would spend hours looking at him, speaking with him, dealing with him in simplicity and veneration. If we turn to our heavenly mother, we will soon learn to speak, with full trust, to Jesus and to follow him closely.

[30] *The Way*, no. 368.
[31] *Furrow*, no. 464.

# Children of God As Apostles

## Christ works through Christians

Upon becoming a member of Christ, a godly creature does what Jesus did: redeem with him by identifying ourselves with him. Then we become Christ passing once again amid men.[1] "You cannot separate the fact that Christ is God from his role as redeemer. The Word became flesh and came into the world to save all men (see 1 Tim 2:4). Despite all our personal defects and limitations, we are other Christs, Christ himself, and we too are called to serve all men."[2] There we have the ultimate reason for being apostolic: it directly stems from our being children of God.

Incorporated to Christ through baptism and as children of God, we participate in Christ and his mission. In truly identifying ourselves with Christ, we continue his task on earth: bringing God to men and our fellow men to God—all steeped in prayer for them and ourselves. Baptism allows us to partake of Christ's priesthood. The supernatural reality of the common priesthood of all the faithful does not impede our remaining ordinary people, with the outlook proper to lay people living in the world but with a Christian soul. Blessed Josemaría spoke of their combining a "lay outlook" and "priestly soul."

Those faithful called to the *ministerial* priesthood (deacons on up) partake of Christ's priestly mission in a way essentially distinct from what they had before, simply as faithful. But the apostolic charge is the same, universal, something in which all

---

[1] "We can never attribute to ourselves the power of Jesus who is passing by among us. Our Lord is passing by, and he transforms souls. . . . But it is he who does it; not you or I. It is Christ who is passing by." *The Forge*, no. 673.

[2] *Christ Is Passing By*, no. 106.

Christians are involved. This universality is a direct result of our divine filiation. "Being children of God transforms us into something that goes far beyond our being people who merely put up with each other. Listen to what Christ says, *Vos autem dixi amicos!* We are friends who, like him, give our lives for each other, when heroism is needed and throughout our ordinary lives."[3]

Apostolic concern stems from Christ's interest in each and every soul. Therefore, "the apostolate of giving doctrine usually has to be, as it were, capillary, spreading from one to another, from each believer to his immediate companion. The children of God care about all souls, because every soul is important."[4] As children of God we cannot turn our backs on those who still do not know Christ. Holiness is not a strictly private affair, something exclusive, since holiness cannot be separated from winning others for God.[5]

Since a Christian is God's child, his apostolic desires will expand till they are as fruitful as Christ's. He is the vine, we are the branches. We will yield fruit in him and glory to his Father and our Father God to the extent we are united to Jesus. A clear sign of our living God's very life in Christ is the apostolic results accompanying children of God. This fruit turns into joy, when we see Christ's words fulfilled: "By this my Father is glorified, that you bear much fruit, and so prove to be my disciples" (Jn 15: 8).

## All apostles, bar none

Spiritual outreach is not just one more thing added to a Christian's many ordinary tasks. Nor is it connected with our constant effort to imitate Christ. Rather it is supernatural overflow: we see souls as Christ did, with a merciful heart, to the degree we identify ourselves with him. It is not an additional chore; much less is it something to be left to specialists, as if only some were soul experts tucked away in a remote corner of the Church. All God's children must get involved, echoing Christ's

---

[3] *Furrow*, no. 750.
[4] Ibid., no. 943.
[5] See *Christ Is Passing By*, no. 145.

ardent commitment. Just as human life and reality can and should occasion conversation, prayer, with God, so should human endeavors be fertilized by Jesus' love. "For a Christian, apostolate is like breathing. A child of God cannot live without this supernatural life-force."[6]

Who isn't loved madly by God? No one can be excluded. God is love, boundless love. He loves each of us as if we alone were the only creature on earth. "He came on earth to redeem everyone, because 'he wishes all men to be saved' (1 Tim 2: 4). There is not a single soul in whom Christ is not interested. Each soul has cost him the price of his blood (see 1 Pt 1: 18–19)."[7]

That is why we are to respect and love absolutely everyone. We are to love them not for their behavior, but because of who they are. If we find ourselves alongside someone who behaves badly or in ways unworthy of Christian dignity, we are to love him as well. "That life that seems so mean is sacred. Christ has died to save it. If he did not despise it, how can you dare to?"[8] He refused to "break a bruised reed" (Mt 12: 20). Are we to do so now?

## Apostles on the job

"If you love the Lord, you will *necessarily* become aware of the blessed burden of souls that need to be brought to God."[9] So did Blessed Josemaría often teach, being well experienced in the impossibility of loving God while not loving God's children. If work can be made into prayer, why can't it also be made apostolic? Surely this divine task is woven into the unity of life forged by the Holy Spirit. "Apostolic concern . . . is not something separate from [Christians'] everyday work. It is part and parcel of one's work, which becomes a source of opportunities for meeting Christ. As we work at our job, side by side with our colleagues, friends, and relatives and sharing their interests, we can help them come closer to Christ."[10] Our heart

[6] Ibid., no. 122.
[7] *Friends of God*, no. 256.
[8] *Furrow*, no. 760.
[9] *The Forge*, no. 63.
[10] *Friends of God*, no. 264.

is then flooded with the same sentiments Christ had: "When he saw the crowds, he had compassion for them, because they were harassed and helpless, like sheep without a shepherd" (Mt 9: 36).

An apostle must work at it, not sparing himself exhaustion. "We have no right to forget that each of us is a worker, one among many, on this plantation where he has placed us to cooperate in the task of providing food for others."[11] With God's help we will not shirk our duty. First and foremost we are to take refuge in him. Then, "every day . . . you will be closer to your brothers."[12] The closer one gets to God, the closer one gets to others. But, throughout, the same condition holds: being close to Jesus, imitating him, becoming him through interior life.

For most children of God, this apostolic commission is to be carried out amid the world, since that is where God wants us to be. "Yes, right there in our work, in our own home, or on the street, with all the small or big problems that arise daily. Right there, not withdrawn from those things, but with our heart fixed on God. . . . Besides, who ever said that to speak about Christ and to spread his doctrine, you need to do anything unusual or remarkable? Just live your ordinary life; work at your job, trying to fulfill the duties of your state in life, doing your job, your professional work properly, improving, getting better each day. Be loyal; be understanding with others and demanding on yourself. Be mortified and cheerful. This will be your apostolate. Then, though you will not see why, because you are very aware of your own wretchedness, you will find that people come to you. Then you can talk to them, quite simply and naturally —on your way home from work, for instance, or in a family gathering, on a bus, walking down the street, anywhere. You will chat about the sort of longings that everyone feels deep down in his soul, even though some people may not want to pay attention to them: they will come to understand them better, when they begin to look for God in earnest."[13]

[11] Ibid., no. 49.
[12] *Furrow*, no. 681.
[13] *Friends of God*, nos. 271, 273.

# Restore all things in Christ

"For he must reign" (1 Cor 15: 25). The Apostle teaches that Christ's sovereignty over all creation has been achieved not in time but will reach its lasting fullness after the universal judgment. St. Paul presents this event, mysterious still for us, as an act of solemn homage to the Father. Christ will offer all creation as a trophy: he will entrust to his Father the kingdom previously entrusted to the Word (see 1 Cor 15: 23–28). His glorious return at the end of time, having established "the new heaven and the new earth" (Rev 21: 1), is tantamount to his final victory over the devil, sin, suffering, and death.

Meanwhile, a child of God participates in Christ's kingship by struggling to sanctify society: "He must reign!" Jesus must reign, above all, in our mind, will, and heart, lest some other love usurp our love for God. He must reign in our body, temple of the Holy Spirit,[14] in our work, road to holiness. . . .

We are called and spurred, so that all around us Christ's loving spirit may impregnate all earthly realities. "Far from diminishing our concern to develop this earth," says Vatican II, "the expectancy of a new earth should spur us on, for it is here that the body of a new human family grows, foreshadowing in some way the age which is to come. That is why, although we must be careful to distinguish earthly progress clearly from the increase of the kingdom of Christ, such progress is of vital concern to the kingdom of God, insofar as it can contribute to the better ordering of human society.

"When we have spread on earth the fruits of our nature and our enterprise—human dignity, brotherly communion, and freedom—we will find them once again, cleansed this time from the stain of sin, illuminated and transfigured, when Christ presents to his Father an eternal and universal kingdom. . . . Here on earth the kingdom is mysteriously present; when the Lord comes it will enter into its perfection."[15] We contribute to the expansion of Christ's kingdom when we try to make both more human and Christian the mission entrusted to us, our daily tasks.

[14] See Pius XI, *Quas primas*, December 11, 1925.
[15] *Gaudium et spes*, no. 39.

It is up to each of us Christians now to make fruitful the treasure of graces God has deposited in our hands. This is the great challenge facing God's children: using all our might to pervade all human sectors with Christian spirit. Nothing is alien to God, for all things have been created by him and are oriented to him, while retaining their own autonomy: business, politics, family, recreation, teaching. . . . The kingdom restored by Christ is at work in the Christian and leads him to be like yeast and a sign of salvation to make the world more just, more brotherly, more cooperative, inspired in the gospel values of hope and future bliss, to which we are all called. "That is the calling of Christians, that is our apostolic task, the desire that should consume our soul: to make this kingdom of Christ a reality, to eliminate hatred and cruelty, to spread throughout the earth the strong and soothing balm of love."[16] This goal can be reached only by drawing many to Jesus: we are to be effective and habitual apostles among the people who cross our path every day.

## Joy and apostolate

If we imitate Christ, no soul can be indifferent to us, for we look on the world "with the very eyes of Christ."[17] We are to look on others with a pitying heart, much as our Teacher does. With the naturalness of a neighbor, an acquaintance, Christ goes about attracting followers, friends, with whom to share his saving message.

By consistently behaving naturally, hiding neither our weaknesses nor our struggle to resemble Christ, we offer those at our side an attractive witness. "They will ask us: Why are you so happy? How do you manage to overcome selfishness and comfort-seeking? Who has taught you to understand others, to live well, and to spend yourself in serving others? Then we must disclose to them the divine secret of Christian existence. We must speak to them about God, Christ, the Holy Spirit, Mary. The time has come for us to use our poor words to communicate the depth of God's love that grace has poured into our souls."[18]

[16] *Christ Is Passing By*, no. 183.
[17] John Paul II, *Redemptor hominis*, no. 18.
[18] *Christ Is Passing By*, no. 148.

For children of God, the apostolic motivation is chiefly a bounty of both supernatural and human joy: to transmit the happiness born of being close to God. When this bliss "overflows onto others, it brings forth hope, optimism, generous impulses amid daily tiredness, eventually infecting all of society. Only if you possess within the divine grace, both peace and joy, will you be able to build something valuable for humanity," affirms John Paul II.[19]

We are especially bound to spread joy within the family. The key characteristic within the home has to be a habitual smile, however tired and preoccupied we may be. This optimistic, cordial, loving way of behaving is like "the stone fallen into the lake."[20] At first it produces a small circular ripple and then a bigger one . . . thus creating a pleasant, contagious atmosphere, which fosters fellowship and where, with naturalness, apostolic benefits reach children, parents, siblings. "The cheerfulness of a man or woman of God has to overflow: it has to be calm, contagious, attractive . . . ; in a few words, it has to be supernatural and natural, so infectious that it may bring others to follow Christian ways."[21]

On the contrary, abrupt, intolerant, pessimistic attitudes distance us from others and God, provoke new tensions, and easily lead to annulling any charity. St. Thomas Aquinas claims that no one can put up with someone sad and petulant even for just a day; therefore each of us is obliged by a social debt to get along cheerfully with others.[22] Overcoming fickle feelings, tiredness, personal worries will always be the usual standard of someone who chooses to be close to God. "You should make sure that wherever you are there is that *good humor*—that cheerfulness—which is born of an interior life."[23]

Deeply grounded in divine filiation, this cheerful, optimistic, smiling spirit is to be brought to one's friends and neighbors, even those with whom we have only a brief encounter. There is the client we will never see again, the patient who, once well,

---

[19] Address, April 10, 1979.
[20] *The Way*, no. 831.
[21] *Furrow*, no. 60.
[22] *Summa Theologiae*, II-II, q. 114, a. 2 ad 2.
[23] *The Forge*, no. 151.

will no longer need a physician, the person who stops us on the street for directions. . . . In the end they will be lifted by our pleasant manner, plus our having prayed to their guardian angel. There will be many who find in a Christian's joy the path leading to God, which otherwise they may never have found. We have often experienced the truth of what Blessed Josemaría says: "The first step toward bringing others to the ways of Christ is for them to see you happy and serene, sure in your advance toward God." [24]

"What must the cheerful way that Jesus looked upon people have been like? It must have been the same that shone from the eyes of his Mother, who could not contain her joy—*Magnificat anima mea Dominum*—and her soul glorified the Lord while she carried him within her and by her side. O Mother! May we, like you, rejoice to be with him and to hold him." [25]

From our Lady we learn how to be useful to others, thinking of their needs, easing both their life here on earth and their path to heaven. She points the way: "Amid the rejoicing at the feast in Cana, only Mary notices that they are short of wine. A soul will notice even the smallest details of service if, like her, it is alive with a passion to help its neighbor, for God." [26] Then how easily we discover God coming to meet us and saying "as you did it to one of the least of these my brethren, you did it to me" (Mt 25: 40).

"A sincere resolution: to make the way lovable and easy for others." [27]

[24] Ibid., no. 858.
[25] *Furrow*, no. 95.
[26] Ibid., no. 631.
[27] Ibid., no. 63.

# CHAPTER 14

# Joy, Suffering, and Death
# for Children of God

## The root of joy

Joy, we are told, is a state arising from the possession of a good or at least the hope of enjoying the good. The will is attracted to various goods discovered by our mind, yet it also displays an unwillingness to settle for anything less than supreme goodness. The satisfaction from achieving lesser goods is as temporary as the craving itself. When one achieves a desired good, the initial enjoyment soon gives way to the dissatisfaction of having a new desire for something else unpossessed. No one seems to be able to settle for mere earthly goods, however satisfying. It is sad that souls try to do so with fleeting goods (an ultimately impossible venture), a sure sign of spiritual poverty. To predicate one's joy and hopes on health, beauty, pleasure, professional success, money, even in the best of cases, falls far short of the heart's capacity, unable to settle for anything less than God. Such limited goods always deceive; they cannot give what they do not have. The desire for bliss "is of divine origin: God has placed it in the human heart in order to draw man to the One who alone can fulfill it. . . . 'God alone satisfies.'"[1]

## Anticipating heaven's bliss

Possessing love and thus joy can begin here on earth, thanks to the grace making us children of God. Full, definitive bliss,

---

[1] *Catechism of the Catholic Church*, no. 1718; Thomas Aquinas, *Expos. in symb. apost.*, I.

which satisfies without satiating, awaits us only in heaven. The mixture of optimism and deprivation that arises from hoping for a good turns to sadness when its possession is thwarted. How disgustedly are prizeless lottery tickets torn up; what a waste of money! Sadness arises from losing a good. "Why do we become dejected? It is because life on earth does not go the way we had hoped, or because obstacles arise that prevent us from satisfying our personal ambitions."[2]

There can be no greater earthly good than savoring the meaning of our divine filiation. In heaven, like an iron filing that finally adheres to the beckoning magnet, we shall see God face to face, ecstatic forever over his goodness and beauty. We shall then understand the whole God but not completely (*totum sed non totaliter*, say theologians), because we are limited. Then, in heaven, we will attain the full joy that God graciously bestows on us. That hope fills our earthly journey with joy. Furthermore, we already partake of an incipient possession of God, which can continue to grow on this side of the grave. "If we feel we are beloved children of our heavenly Father, as indeed we are, how can we fail to be happy all the time?"[3]

In heaven, children of God achieve perfect fullness; here on earth, children of God are on the way to that fullness. Our cheerfulness is rooted in this, for it "is a necessary consequence of our divine filiation, of knowing that our Father God loves us as his favorites, that he holds us up and helps us and forgives us."[4] He quiets our restless heart with love.

Let us be children of God and dwell often on this reality throughout the day. Sadder than tearing up some useless lottery tickets would be throwing away our ever-rewarding divine filiation, perhaps by not considering it enough. To be a child and to live like a slave would be disgraceful. Blessed Josemaría would insist: "Be cheerful, always cheerful. It is for those to be sad who do not consider themselves to be children of God."[5] For the

[2] *Friends of God*, no. 108.

[3] *The Forge*, no. 266.

[4] Ibid., no. 332.

[5] *Furrow*, no. 54. "Some people feel embittered all the time. Everything makes them uneasy. They go to sleep with a physical obsession: that this sleep, the only possible escape, is not going to last very long. They wake up with the unwelcome and disheartening feeling that they now have another day in front of them.

love of God we should struggle to reject sad, pessimistic moods. We are children of God, after all.

There can be no deeper joy in this life, because nothing can compare with the boundless treasure of belonging to the divine Family. Losing this familiarity with God for all eternity will lead to infinite sadness. An ineffable pain must follow on having forfeited, by means of grave sin, one's condition as a good and faithful child.[6]

Growing in divine filiation also bolsters our joy. Because ours is an unlimited capacity to be children of God, so too is our bliss limitless. The more we feel and act like children of God, the more we experience joy from this divine intimacy here on earth. "How beautiful our Christian vocation is—to be children of God! It brings joy and peace on earth that the world cannot give."[7]

Even amid conflict, divine filiation bestows on us a serene well-being, far superior to any earthly satisfactions. "Words have not yet been invented to express all that one feels—in the heart and in the will—when one knows oneself to be a child of God."[8] Why? Because the supernatural mystery of our divine filiation leaves us wordless, for we are left awash in a joy and serenity "that come from the abandonment of everything, including oneself, into the loving arms of our Father God."[9]

---

Many have forgotten that the Lord has placed us in the world on our way to eternal happiness. They do not realize that only those who walk on earth with the joy of children of God will be able to attain it." Ibid., no. 305.

[6] "For a Christian, joy is a treasure. Only by offending God do we lose it, because sin is the fruit of selfishness, and selfishness is the root of sadness. Even then, a bit of joy survives under the debris of our soul: the knowledge that neither God nor his Mother can ever forget us. If we repent, if an act of sorrow springs from our heart, if we purify ourselves in the holy sacrament of penance, God comes out to meet and forgive us. Then there can be no sadness whatsoever. Then there is every right 'to rejoice, because your brother was dead and has come back to life, was lost and has been found' (Lk 15:32)." *Christ Is Passing By*, no. 178. Sacramental confession is truly the sacrament of joy.

[7] *The Forge*, no. 269.

[8] *Furrow*, no. 61.

[9] *The Way*, no. 659.

## Joy despite troubles and weakness

As we confront our own shortcomings, which seemingly increase at almost every turn, the joy children of God experience sometimes becomes clouded. Yet for a child of God, weaknesses are also a reason to rejoice. They offer an occasion to experience our Father God's mercy and goodness. Mothers are thrilled to give to their newborns all the care that is needed, and then some, with no repugnance at the helpless child's limitations. They teach the young child to talk, to read, and to pray; they would truly suffer if the child were foolishly to try to be independent. The fact that a toddler needs practically everything spurs his mother's love and generosity. If they truly love their parents, good children show they need them.

But in the spiritual realm there is no need for airs: we weaklings are always in need of God, in everything. And he loves us "just as we are," insisted Blessed Josemaría, that is, weak, fragile, barely worth anything. That is why he wrote: "To know we are made of clay, [the broken pieces] riveted together again, is a continual source of joy. It means acknowledging our littleness in the eyes of God: a little child. Can there be any joy to compare with that of the person who, knowing himself to be poor and weak, knows also that he or she is a child of God?" [10] When we feel our weakest and neediest is when we are to revel all the more in our divine filiation.

The peerless joy born of being and knowing oneself to be a child of God does not rest on our virtues, on the satisfaction of right-doing, but solely on our helplessness. Thereon does God build joy. "Don't be afraid to know your real self. That's right, you are made of clay. Don't be worried. For you and I are children of God. . . . We are chosen by a divine calling from all eternity: 'The Father chose us in Christ before the foundation of the world, that we should be holy and blameless before him' (Eph 1: 4)." [11]

Such is our life: struggling to please our Father, giving him joys, like his Son Jesus Christ, in whom he is well pleased. That is the reason for the cheerfulness in the lives of children of God,

[10] *Friends of God*, no. 108.
[11] *Christ Is Passing By*, no. 160.

trying to behave as such.[12] External adversities, obstacles, unfairnesses, misunderstandings, and the like are in themselves unable to wrestle away our gladness and serenity. Such is the true realism born of faith. "Christian teaching on pain is not a series of facile considerations. It is, in the first place, a call to accept the suffering inseparable from all human life."[13] So long as the cause lasts, the effect will remain. If joy stems from divine filiation, and because this cannot disappear, joy will remain. Only grave sin weakens our filiation. So long as we consequently struggle, our cheerfulness cannot end.

## Pain makes us resemble Christ

If personal shortcomings cannot diminish our joy as children of God, we are also to discover how physical or spiritual setbacks can contribute to our joy. "You asked me if I had a cross to bear. And I answered, 'Yes, we always have to bear the cross.' But it is a glorious cross, a divine seal, the authentic guarantee of our being children of God. That is why, with the cross, we always travel happily on our way."[14] That is how the Holy Spirit shapes us into Christ.

The chisel's blows cause pain, as did the nails through our Lord's body. "But that suffering is our purification; the sweat and the blood that disfigure and tarnish his features serve to cleanse us."[15] Suffering is what purifies and identifies us with Jesus: "Lord, help me decide to tear off, through penance, this pitiful mask I have fashioned with my wretched doings. . . . Then, and only then, by following the path of contemplation and atonement, will my life begin to copy faithfully the features of your life. We will find ourselves more and more like you. We will be other Christs, Christ himself: *ipse Christus*."[16]

---

[12] "Joy is a Christian possession that we will have as long as we keep fighting, for it is a consequence of peace. Peace is the fruit of having conquered in war, and the life of man upon this earth, as we read in sacred scripture, is a warfare." *The Forge,* no. 105.

[13] *Christ Is Passing By*, no. 168.

[14] *Furrow*, no. 70.

[15] *The Way of the Cross*, sixth station.

[16] Ibid.

It is faith, supernatural outlook, that sees God's loving hand behind everything, that turns the "cross" into Christ's holy cross, one befitting children of God. And that is where we always find the cause of joy, because it identifies us with him and readies us to live with him the glory of his resurrection.[17] Christ's cross is not the pain and restlessness brought on by self-love, envy, laziness. . . .

The joy born of identifying ourselves with Christ, therefore with pain, and even dishonor, moved Blessed Josemaría Escrivá to say: "Listen to me, my child: you must be happy when people treat you badly and dishonor you, when many come out against you, and it becomes the done thing to spit on you, because you are *omnium peripsema*: like the refuse of the world.

"It's hard, it's very hard. It is hard until at last one goes to the tabernacle, seeing oneself thought of as the scum of the earth, like a wretched worm, and says with all one's heart, 'Lord, if you don't need my good name, what do I want it for?' Up to then— to the point of nakedness and giving—even a child of God does not know what happiness is. It is the self-giving of love, but it is founded on mortification, on sorrow."[18]

Adverse circumstances neither determine nor threaten true joy. "How can one be happy when faced with sickness or injustice? In those straits wouldn't joy be a mirage or an irresponsible escape mechanism? Not at all! Christ, and only he, gives us the answer. . . . On the cross, he accepts suffering to make us happy. He thus teaches us that, united to him, we can also give a saving value to pain and thus turn it into joy. Ours is to be the deepest joy born of sacrificing ourselves for the sake of others and of making reparation for one's own and others' sins.

"In the light of Christ's cross, therefore, there is no room for fearing pain, because we understand that love is shown through suffering: our authentic love of God and of all humanity."[19] Joy

[17] The Lord's cross is not found in what is disagreeable as such. That's a mistake calling for clarification. "There is a kind of fear around, a fear of the cross, of our Lord's cross. What has happened is that people have begun to regard as crosses all the unpleasant things that crop up in life, and they do not know how to take them as God's children should, with supernatural outlook." *The Way of the Cross*, second station, no. 5.

[18] *The Forge*, no. 803.

[19] Avillo del Portillo, Homily at World Youth Day, April 12, 1984.

disappears only when we stray from God through sin, luke-warmness, reluctance to deal with God, or unenlightenedly revolving around ourselves. We also forfeit it when we refuse the cross that can assume many faces: sorrow, illness, failure, setbacks, disruption of plans, humiliations. . . . "Christians, if they really behave as God's children, will suffer discomfort, heat, tiredness, cold. . . . But they will never lack joy, because that, all that, is ordained or permitted by him who is the source of true happiness." [20]

Divine filiation gives the deepest meaning to our life, even to suffering. Everything happens by will of our loving Father; consequently from each situation we can draw great benefits. "Woes? Setbacks deriving from one thing or another? Can't you see that this is the will of your Father God, who is good and who loves you—loves *you* personally—more than all the mothers in the world can possibly love their children?" [21] This is how a child of God sees beyond the here and now and understands with a new awareness what occupies him currently. He understands that our reality as children of God has far to go before being consummated in glory.

Meanwhile, "all those who love find that their life is a forge, a forging in the fire of sorrow. There, in that forge, our Lord teaches us that those who tread fearlessly where the Master treads, hard though the going is, find joy." [22] Has any saint ever been sad?

## Death: final encounter with Christ

Divine filiation also changes the meaning of death, the hardest and most difficult challenge awaiting us. Death comes to us via original sin. "God did not make death" (Wis 1: 15). Before that first sin there was no death, not as we know it; we have often seen it surrounded by sorrow and hardship. Now, to reach the Father's house, we must go through that gate: "to depart out of this world to the Father" (Jn 13: 1), to our Father. But Jesus

[20] *Furrow*, no. 82.
[21] *The Forge*, no. 929.
[22] Ibid., no. 816.

Christ "abolished death and brought life and immortality to light" (2 Tim 1: 10); he removed its essential badness, its sting. Thanks to him, death acquires a meaning new to God's children: it is but a step to a new life, to God's life made ours as his children.

"I am," said the Teacher, "the resurrection and the life; he who believes in me, though he die, yet shall he live, and whoever lives and believes in me shall never die" (Jn 11: 25). The godless keep on living as if Christ had not redeemed us, not knowing themselves to be God's children. No wonder when facing death they tremble and anguish. "Evil shall slay the wicked" (Ps 34: 21), while "precious in the sight of the Lord is the death of his saints" (Ps 116: 15); for God's children it is their *dies natalis*: the day when they radiantly gaze on Jesus' face. "Only unloving children do not look forward to meeting their parents."[23]

We are only visiting here. "Death comes and cannot be avoided. What empty vanity it is, then, to center our existence on this life. See how much many men and women suffer. Some suffer because life is coming to an end and it pains them to leave it; others, because it keeps going and they're sick of it. In neither case is there room for the mistaken view that makes our passage through the world an end in itself.

"One must leave that way of thinking behind and anchor oneself to another, an eternal one. A total change is required, to empty oneself of self-centered motives, which pass away, and to be renewed in Christ, who is eternal."[24] We are considering just that "total change," which presupposes being "renewed in Christ," to live this new "way of thinking" as do children of God.

"Many people have spoken to me in amazement of the joy which, thanks be to God, my children in Opus Dei have and which they spread to others. Faced with this evident truth, I always give the same reply, because I know no other. Their happiness has its foundation in the fact that they fear neither life nor death; that they are not overwhelmed when they meet with misfortune; that they strive daily to live with a spirit of sacrifice,

[23] *Furrow*, no. 885.
[24] Ibid., no. 879.

in spite of their own defects and weaknesses, and they are constantly ready to deny themselves in order to make the Christian path easier and more pleasant for others."[25] Thus did he summarize the life of a child of God: fearing "neither life nor death."[26]

Throughout life sorrow makes itself felt; no existence is exempt from it; the end of our earthly sojourn is visited by it. But by embracing sufferings out of love, we identify ourselves with Christ. "Don't be afraid of death. Accept it from this day on, generously . . . when God wills it, how God wills it, where God wills it. Believe me, it will come at the time, in the place, and in the way that are best—sent by your Father God. May our sister death be welcome!"[27]

From our Father's hand we welcome death peacefully, even with joy. "When you think about death, do not be afraid, in spite of your sins. For he already knows that you love him and what stuff you are made of. If you seek him, he will welcome you as the father welcomed the prodigal son; but you have to seek him."[28]

Interior life, built on seeking our Father God, has taken place amid habitual encounters with God, amid humble repenting, amid the blows that have sculpted Christ's image in our soul, and amid caresses from divine hands. So, after this life, just a short dream, and since our Father God loves us so much, he will give us a good awakening, if we do not resist.[29] This childlike perspective should also color God's judgment awaiting us. "Doesn't your soul burn with the desire to make your Father God happy when he has to judge you?"[30]

[25] *Friends of God*, no. 132.

[26] "A child of God fears neither life nor death, because his spiritual life is founded on a sense of divine filiation. So he says to himself: God is my Father and he is the author of all good; he is all-goodness." *The Forge*, no. 987.

[27] *The Way*, no. 739.

[28] *Furrow*, no. 880.

[29] See *The Way*, no. 692.

[30] Ibid., no. 746.

# Our glorious homecoming

When ruminating about death, a child of God enjoys the certainty of hope, as he considers, "What will it be like when all the infinite beauty and greatness, and happiness and love of God will be poured into the poor clay vessel that a human being is, to satisfy it eternally with the freshness of an ever new joy?" [31]

Christ foretold us: "I go to prepare a place for you" (Jn 14: 2). There in heaven we have our house forevermore, right next to Jesus and his most holy Mother. Here we are but pilgrims. "We never die—death is but a change of house. Along with faith and love, we Christians have this hope, a certain hope. We only say, 'So long.' How do we take leave of our loved ones when we die? 'Till we meet again.'" [32] Later, if we are faithful, we will all be reunited.

Now it is not easy to imagine what our heavenly life will be like, the "promised land," where there will be no thirst or tiredness. All good things will abound. "They shall not hunger or thirst, neither scorching wind nor sun shall smite them, for he who has pity on them will lead them, and by springs of water will guide them" (Is 49: 10). Jesus insisted time and again that ours will be perfect, everlasting bliss. It is one of the promises the faithful most like to hear: eternal beatitude is compared, among many other images, to a banquet God has prepared (see Lk 13: 29), where souls can completely satisfy their desire for happiness.

"Beloved, we are God's children now; it does not yet appear what we shall be, but we know that when he appears we shall be like him, for we shall see him as he is" (1 Jn 3: 2). Heaven will be the peak of filiation, of our living in God, an ineffable fullness that begins in our living his life by means of sanctifying grace.

The soul and its powers, plus the body, once resurrected, by virtue of filiation, will be deified, while respecting the infinite distance between creature and Creator. Besides contemplating God as he is himself, his children will most perfectly see in God the features most related to them. This knowledge will add to their joy. They clearly perceive everything pertaining to the

---

[31] *Furrow*, no. 891.

[32] Josemaría Escrivá, *Hoja informativa para la causa de beatificación*, no. 1, p. 5.

world's beauty and wholeness, as part of the universe. As members of the human community, they know what on earth was the object of God's interest and love. Raised by both grace and glory, theirs will be a clear knowledge, though still limited, of God's salvific designs: the Incarnation, Mary's motherhood, the Church. . . .

In heaven we will see our Father God face to face. We shall enjoy him with boundless euphoria, in keeping with the holiness and merits accumulated here on earth. But God's mercy is so great that his children have further cause for bliss in the company of the God-man, whom we shall see in his glorious body. We will recognize him after all those heartfelt conversations with him. . . . There also will be the Virgin, St. Joseph, all the angels (especially our very own guardian angel), and all the saints. How joyful we will be to meet again those we most loved on earth: parents, brothers and sisters, friends . . . those who decisively contributed to our salvation. . . . We will find further cause for rejoicing in the arrival of new souls to heaven, the spiritual progress of loved ones still on earth, the fruits of apostolic efforts throughout the centuries. . . . This "accidental glory" will wax till the very day of universal judgment. Then, our soul will be reunited with our very own body, now raised and glorious, for the soul was created to be the body's form.

Meanwhile, a good child rejoices especially when, facing life's daily troubles, he thinks of his Father God. "With the knowledge of its own wretchedness, it utters with a fruitful desire that Pauline exclamation: *Non vivo ego*—it is no longer I who live, but Christ who lives in me. And he will live forever." [33]

[33] *Furrow*, no. 892.

# CHAPTER 15

# The Conversion of God's Children

## Our weak condition

"You are discouraged, why? Is it your sins and miseries? Is it your defeats, at times coming one after the other? A really big fall, which you didn't expect? Be simple; open your heart. Look: as yet nothing has been lost. You can still go forward, and with more love, with more affection, with more strength.

"Take refuge in your divine filiation: God is your most loving Father. In this lies your security, the haven where you can drop anchor, no matter what is happening on the surface of the sea of life. And you will find joy, strength, optimism: victory!"[1] Seeing ourselves as children of God is our main strength in all situations.

Life's path is a trail leading ever upward to God, ending in heaven. It all got under way with the advent of grace, which erased original sin and made us God's children. But left behind was a tendency to sin, our mind still somewhat obscure and our will still weak. "We carry within us a principle of opposition, of resistance to grace. It comes from the wounds inflicted by original sin and is aggravated by our own personal sins. Therefore, we have to strive ever upward, by means of our everyday tasks, which are both divine and human and always lead to love of God. In this we must be humble and contrite of heart, and we must trust in God's help, while at the same time devoting our best efforts to those tasks as if everything depended on us.

"As we fight this battle, which will last until the day we die, we cannot exclude the possibility that enemies both within and without may attack with violent force. And, as if this burden were not enough, you may at times be assailed by the memory

[1] *The Way of the Cross*, seventh station, no. 2.

of your own past errors, which may have been very many. I tell you now, in God's name: don't despair. Should this happen (it need not happen; nor will it usually happen), then turn it into another motive for uniting yourself more closely to our Lord, for he has chosen you as his child and he will not abandon you. He has allowed that trial to befall you, so that you may love him the more and may discover even more clearly his constant protection and love."[2]

We are constantly threatened by the devil, the father of lies. If we do something bad, he suggests that there is no remedy. If we act well, he whispers that we are practically saints. Thus if, thanks to God's mercy, we keep ascending to him, we would deceive ourselves if we were to think "that our longing to seek Christ, and the fact that we are meeting him and getting to know him and enjoy the sweetness of his love, makes us incapable of sinning."[3] Habitual erring, sincerely made resolves left unfulfilled, weaknesses: these ought not catch us off guard. "We should not be surprised to find, in our body or soul, the needle of pride, sensuality, envy, laziness, and the desire to dominate others. This is a fact of life, proven by personal experience. It is the point of departure and the normal context for winning in this intimate sport, this race toward our Father's house."[4]

So then, we are neither sinless nor capable of fully realizing how sinful we are. Given our weak human condition, God the Father plays the role of a physician tending the sick who need him. In us God's mercy finds plenty of shortcomings wherein to prove his healing power, applying the remedy that leads us back to the Father. God thus displays his prowess, and he "spurs us on to fight, to battle against our defects, although we know that we will never achieve total victory during our pilgrimage on earth. The Christian life is a continuous beginning again each day. It renews itself over and over."[5] Keeping this reality before our eyes is essential to our not losing hope.

We are to keep up this struggle of gentle, habitual tension. Ours should be a constant conversion, one of humble repen-

---

[2] *Friends of God*, no. 214.
[3] Ibid., no. 303.
[4] *Christ Is Passing By*, no. 75.
[5] Ibid., no. 114.

tance, which does not undermine our personality but rather reinforces it. We are to keep on ascending to the summit that is Christ, converting defeats into victories.

## Sacrament of mercy

When we have abused God's love, failing as a child to venerate him, "awareness that God is our Father brings joy to our conversion: it tells us we are returning to our Father's house."[6] The disgrace brought about by having grieved our Father God opens the door to humility, love, and trust.

Although our weakness makes itself felt on every side, we should fear nothing, so long as we repent and make amends for our sins. "Men do not scandalize God. He can put up with all our infidelities. Our heavenly Father pardons any offense when his child returns to him, when he repents and asks for pardon."[7] When we strive to please God, "what does it matter that we stumble on the way, if we find in the pain of our fall the energy to pick ourselves up and go on with renewed vigor? Don't forget that the saint is not the person who never falls, but rather one who never fails to get up again, humbly with a holy stubbornness."[8]

Returning to God on the heels of conversion and penance is not an isolated event in Christian life. Ours is to be a constant conversion, rooted essentially in these two realities: our frailty and the consoling truth of our divine filiation. Therefore, in the battle for holiness, "we should not be depressed by our falls, not even by serious falls, if we go to God in the sacrament of penance contrite and resolved to improve. A Christian is not a neurotic collector of good behavior reports. Jesus Christ our Lord was moved as much by Peter's repentance after his fall as by John's innocence and faithfulness. Jesus understands our weakness and draws us to himself on an inclined plane. He wants us to make an effort to climb a little each day. He seeks us out, just as he did the disciples of Emmaus, whom he went out to meet.

[6] Ibid., no. 64.
[7] Ibid.
[8] *Friends of God*, no. 131.

He sought Thomas, showed himself to him, and made him touch with his fingers the open wounds in his hands and side. Jesus Christ is always waiting for us to return to him; he knows our weakness." [9]

In confession what had been the origin of sadness and sterility is turned into a fountain of life. The sacrament of penance "tenderly manifests divine goodness, Jesus' mercy, he who is father and brother and knows how to pardon and overlook. How wonderful to kneel down and hear our Lord (for the priest is Christ himself): I absolve you from your sins, I pardon you." [10]

Experienced in the huge benefits deriving from frequent confession, Blessed Josemaría advised: "Go weekly to the holy sacrament of penance, to the sacrament of divine pardon—and as often as necessary, without giving in to scruples. Thus robed in grace, we will pass through the mountains, as told of in the Psalms, and continue upward by fulfilling our Christian duties, without getting distracted. When with goodwill we use these remedies and beg God for an ever greater hope, ours will be the contagious joy of those who know themselves to be children of God. 'If God is for us, who is against us?' (Rom 8: 31). Our radical transformation into Christ takes place in the sacrament of mercy. There, besides recovering the fullness of our filial condition lost owing to grave sin, is bolstered our sorrow of love, a contrition that identifies us with Christ." [11]

God always hears us; he is always ready to come into our lives, to free us from evil, and to fill us with goodness, with the joy that stems from communion with him. Jesus himself explained the parable of the prodigal son, underscoring the joy of God the

---

[9] *Christ Is Passing By*, no. 75.

[10] Josemaría Escrivá, *Hoja informativa*, no. 5, p. 4. "If you should stray from him for any reason, react with the humility that will lead you to begin again and again; to play the role of the prodigal son every day and even repeatedly during the twenty-four hours of the same day; to correct your contrite heart in confession, which is a real miracle of God's love. In this wonderful sacrament our Lord cleanses your soul and fills you with joy and strength to prevent you from giving up the fight, and to help you keep returning to God unwearied, when everything seems black. In addition, the Mother of God, who is also our mother, watches over you with motherly care, guiding your every step." *Friends of God*, no. 214.

[11] *Hoja informativa*, no. 5, p. 6.

Father and that of the sinner returning to him. "God comes out to meet and forgive us. Then there can be no sadness whatsoever. Then there is every right 'to rejoice, because your brother was dead and has come back to life, was lost and has been found' (Lk 15: 32).

"These words are taken from the marvelous ending of the parable of the prodigal son, which we shall never tire of meditating. 'Behold [the Father] comes out to meet you. He will bend down to greet you. He will give you a kiss as a sign of love and tenderness. He will order the servants to bring you new clothing, a ring, shoes for your feet. You still fear reproach and he returns your dignity. You fear punishment and he gives you a kiss. You dread a harsh word and he prepares for you a banquet.' "[12]

## God's small children

God is especially Father when dispensing mercy in response to our repeated failings. Even when ours are major failures (for we will always have little ones), "we will never hesitate to react and return to the sure path of divine filiation that ends up in the open and welcoming arms of our Father God."[13] And conversant with our wretchedness, we will say with the simplicity of little children: Lord, "allow yourself to be taken in by this child of yours, just like those good fathers, full of kindness, who put into the hands of their little children the presents they want to receive from them—knowing perfectly well that little children have nothing of their own. And what joy father and child have together, even though they are both in on the secret."[14]

Thus the path of spiritual infancy is also a good way to grow in filiation. We will always be helped along by God, even carried in his arms, though many times we will try to take our own steps, however awkward and prone to falls. "In our interior life it does all of us good to be *quasi modo geniti infantes,* like those tiny

[12] *Christ Is Passing By,* no. 178; St. Ambrose, *Expositio Evangelii secundum Lucam,* 7 (PL 15:1540).

[13] *Friends of God,* no. 148.

[14] *The Forge,* no. 195.

tots who seem to be made of rubber and who even enjoy falling over because they get up again right away and are once more running around, and also because they know their parents will always be there to console them, whenever they are needed.

"If we try to act like them, our stumbling and failures in the interior life (which, moreover, are inevitable) will never result in bitterness. Our reaction will be one of sorrow but not discouragement, and we'll smile with a smile that gushes up like fresh water out of the joyous awareness that we are children of that love, that grandeur, that infinite wisdom, that mercy, that is our Father. During the years I have been serving our Lord, I have learned to become like a little child of God. I would ask you to do likewise, to be *quasi modo geniti infantes,* children who long for God's word, his bread, his food, his strength, to enable us to behave henceforth as Christian men and women." [15]

To live with this simplicity we must keep two realities in mind: God's paternal goodness and our mistake-prone weakness. We will blame our falls neither on circumstances nor on the impossibility of doing otherwise; we must accept responsibility for our misdeeds. So, we are to be humble, seeing ourselves as weak and ever in need of help and forgiveness.

How saving is sincerity: "the truth will make you free" (Jn 8: 32), said the Teacher. On the other hand, deceit, duplicity, and falsehood quickly lead to separation from God and to the absence of charitable fruits. The psalmist exclaimed: "My strength was dried up as by the heat of summer" (32: 4).

The root of insincerity is pride, which prevents us from submitting to God, from acknowledging our dependence on him and his will. It also makes it very difficult for us to admit that we have done wrong and to set things right. If insincerity persists, our dispositions sour along with our objectivity. A soul out to dismiss its faults becomes an expert at making excuses. If not avoided, this flirting with falsehood turns into blindness. We consequently need a humble attitude to grow in sincere self-knowledge and to confess our sins and weaknesses. Humility leads us to accept the most radical self-insufficiency and to beg God for forgiveness many times a day for the misdeeds in our life or for those that could have gone better.

[15] *Friends of God,* no. 146.

"Serious falls, of the kind that can do great damage to the soul, at times almost irreparable damage, can always be traced back to the pride of thinking oneself to be grown up and self-sufficient. In such cases, people seem almost incapable of asking for help from those who can give it: not only from God, but also from a friend or from a priest. And the poor soul, alone in its misfortune, sinks into confusion and loses its way."[16] So, then, "don't try to be older. A child, always a child, even when you are dying of old age. When a child stumbles and falls, nobody is surprised; his father promptly picks him up. When the person who stumbles and falls is older, the immediate reaction is one of laughter. Sometimes, after this first impulse, the laughter gives way to pity. But older people have to get up by themselves.

"Your sad experience is that each day is full of stumbles and falls. What would become of you if you were not continually more of a child? Don't try to be older. Be a child, and when you stumble, may your Father God pick you up by the hand."[17] How we need God, and if we let him, he always acts in us, even more so when he sees our awareness of our weakness.

If sometimes it seems as if everything is collapsing about us because we have not behaved as God's children, let us hear the kind reproach of Blessed Josemaría: "But, have you once again forgotten that God is your Father?—all-powerful, infinitely wise, and full of mercy."[18]

If we were to feel especially disheartened by some spiritual ailment that seems incurable, let us not forget that we are God's small children. Then too let us remember Jesus' consoling words: "Those who are well have no need of a physician, but those who are sick" (Mt 9: 12). Everything has its remedy. God

[16] Ibid., no. 147.

[17] *The Way*, no. 870. "You are full of weaknesses. Each day you see them more clearly. But don't let them frighten you. He well knows you can't yield more fruit. Your involuntary falls, those of a child, show your Father God that he must take more care, and your mother Mary that she must never let you go from her loving hand. Each day as our Lord picks you up from the ground, take advantage of it, embrace him with all your strength, and lay your wearied head on his open breast so that you will be carried away by the beating of his most loving heart." Ibid., no. 884.

[18] *The Way of the Cross*, ninth station, no. 4.

is always very close to us, especially when our wretchedness and misdeeds loom.

## Everything is for the best

At one moment during that poignant supper on the last night Jesus spent with his disciples before his Passion and death, he "rose from supper, laid aside his garments, and girded himself with a towel. Then he poured water into a basin, and began to wash the disciples' feet and to wipe them with the towel with which he was girded" (Jn 13: 4ff). The washing continued until he reached Peter, who both showed surprise and reluctance: "Lord, do you wash my feet?" To which Christ replied: "What I am doing you do not know now, but afterward you will understand."

"You do not know now. . . ." Neither do we always understand events permitted by God: pain, illness, bankruptcy, unemployment, the "premature" death of a loved one. . . . God has higher plans, encompassing all of life and eternity. Our mind barely comprehends what is at hand. Often we do not understand even human affairs, though we accept them. Aren't we going to trust our all-provident Lord? Is our confidence in him limited to events acceptable to us? We are entirely in his hands. And what better place could there be? Hereafter God will explain in detail the reason behind so many things we did not understand, so we can see that his all-solicitous hand was behind everything, even the tiniest.

When faced with failure or happenings we cannot decipher, let us try to hear Christ saying, "You do not know now, but afterward you will understand." Then there can be no room for dejection or resentment. When faced with painful events, from the depths of our soul will spring forth a simple, humble, trusting prayer: Lord, you know more; I abandon myself in you; I will understand why later.

St. Paul wrote to the first Christians in Rome (8: 28): *Diligentibus Deum omnia cooperantur in bonum,* "in everything God works for good with those who love him." "Woes? Setbacks deriving from one thing or another? Can't you see that this is the will of your Father God, who is good and who loves you—loves *you* personally—more than all the mothers in the world can possibly love their children?"[19] The instinct of divine filiation will lead us to discover that we are in the hands of a Father who knows the past, the present, and the future and who orchestrates everything solely for our good, even though it is not the thing we sought, owing to our short-sightedness. These considerations should lead us to serenity and peace, even amid the greatest tribulations. That is why we should always follow the advice St. Peter gave to the first faithful: "Cast all your anxieties on him, for he cares about you" (1 Pet 5: 7). No one could possibly take better care of us; God is never mistaken.

In the human realm even those who most care for us err at times, and instead of helping they add to our troubles. That cannot happen with God, who is boundlessly wise and powerful. Always respecting our freedom, he leads us *suaviter et fortiter,* gently but strongly, to what really matters, to eternal happiness. Even our very faults and sins can be for the best, for "God straightens out absolutely everything for the welfare of his children, so that even those who stray and fall he helps to progress in virtue, because they thereby turn more humble and knowing."[20] Contrition steers the soul to a deeper and more trusting love, to greater intimacy with God.

Therefore, to the extent we feel like children of God, life turns into unending thanksgiving. Even behind what seems humanly catastrophic, the Holy Spirit helps us to see "a caress from God," which moves us to be appreciative. Thank you, Lord! we say amid a painful disease or when we learn of a lamentable event. So did the saints react; and we can learn from them how to behave in the face of life's misfortunes. "God is very pleased with those who recognize his goodness by reciting the *Te Deum* in thanksgiving whenever something out of the ordinary happens, without caring whether it may have been good or bad, as the world reckons these things. For everything comes from the hands of our Father; so though the blow of the chisel may hurt our flesh, it is a sign of love, as he smoothes off our rough edges and brings us closer to perfection."[21]

---

[19] *The Forge*, no. 929.
[20] St. Augustine, *On Conversion and grace*, 30.
[21] *The Forge*, no. 609.

Abandonment and trust in God in no way lead us to passivity, wherein there often lurk negligence, laziness, or complicity. We are to fight against physical and moral evils with all the means and might at our command, knowing that our effort, whether fruitful or not, is pleasing to God and the source of many human and supernatural benefits. When sickness strikes, besides accepting it and offering up the pains and suffering in its wake, we are to use all the remedies the case requires: physician, rest, medications. . . . And the injustice, inequalities, and privations experienced by others will lead us Christians, with others of goodwill, to seek the resources and solutions that seem most called for. The same goes for the ignorance and illiteracy, of all kinds, that afflict others. Nothing is more alien to Christian spirit than a misunderstood trust in God that anesthetizes us in the face of others' suffering.

God is our Father who takes exquisite care of us, but he relies on the intelligence and common sense of his children in following the path he points out to us and on the fraternal love at work in us to benefit still others. He has endowed us with certain talents that cannot remain fallow. We hallow ourselves; even when having used the required means, we seem to fail in the absence of the desired result. God sanctifies whatever "failures" result from our conscientious endeavors, but he does not bless omissions. He deals with us as intelligent creatures and expects us to use the adequate means and efforts available.

In each case we will do our best and then *omnia in bonum*, everything for the best! Appearing good or bad, the results will lead us to love God more and never to stray from him. In the spirit of divine filiation, we will find the protection and fatherly warmth that all of us need. So did Blessed Josemaría Escrivá tirelessly teach.

# Bibliography

The Way of the Cross
7th Station, No. 2.